Brewery Adventures
in the Big East

Brewery Adventures in the Big East

Jack Erickson

RedBrick Press

SONOMA, CALIFORNIA

Brewery Advertures in the Big East

Copyright © 1994 by Jack Erickson

RedBrick Press
P.O. Box 1895
Sonoma, California 95476

ISBN: 0-941397-06-8
Library of Congress Catalog Card Number: 94-92240

First Edition
First Printing August 1994

Manufactured in the United States of America
10 9 8 7 6 5 4 3 2 1

To the Tunkis family –
for your hospitality and friendship

Books by Jack Erickson
Published by RedBrick Press

California Brewin'

Brewery Adventures in the Wild West

Great Cooking with Beer

Star Spangled Beer
A Guide to America's New Microbreweries and Brewpubs

≈ TABLE OF CONTENTS ≈

≈ FOREWORD ≈

The Brewery Adventure continues...to the eastern states bordering on the Atlantic Ocean where brewing began almost 400 years ago.

The Brewery Adventures began in 1991 when I published *Brewery Adventures in the Wild West.* The book featured 143 craft breweries in the 13 western states and 2 Canadian provinces where the North American craft brewing revolution was reaching impressive dimensions.

The second Brewery Adventure book, *California Brewin',* appeared in 1993 and focused on the state where craft brewing began. Both books were based on travel and research I did in the West beginning in 1985, where the craft brewing revolution, then called the "microbrewing" revolution, was born. Since 1985, the nascent industry has exploded into a full-blown business and cultural movement that has spread across the entire nation.

There were only about 20 microbreweries in 1985 sprinkled around the West from Helena, Montana, Caldwell, Idaho, and Boulder, Colorado, to San Francisco, Portland, and Seattle. A few had popped up in the Midwest and on the East Coast, but microbreweries took hold in the West first. Fritz Maytag is credited with being the first microbrewer when he bought the failing Anchor Brewery in 1965. Maytag didn't know what he was starting with that rescue of the small San Francisco brewery, but he was planting the first seed of a rebirth of the nation's centuries-old brewing industry.

The second seed was planted a decade later, in 1976, when Jack McAuliffe started New Albion Brewery, in Sonoma, California. The next seeds were planted in the early 1980s, again in the West: Ken Grossman and Paul Camusi started their Sierra Nevada Brewery in Chico, California, in 1981; Bert Grant opened Yakima Brewing and Malting, in Washington, followed by Mendocino Brewing and Buffalo Bill's Brewpub, which opened in 1983 in northern California. The popularity of these pioneering breweries proved that the United States was fertile ground for breweries that had played a significant role in our early history – small breweries making hand-crafted beers for local markets. We were about to discover our brewing heritage. A brewing renaissance had begun. History was being made.

MICROBREWERIES COME EAST

The growth of the West Coast microbreweries was not lost on East Coast entrepreneurs, many of whom visited the first generation of breweries in California, Oregon, Washington, and Colorado. These entrepreneurs went back home and began the arduous task of convincing investors, local zoning officials, and family and friends that microbrewing could flourish in the East as it had in the Wild West. It was just a matter of time. A market for specialty beers had been there for decades, but no one had seen the opportunity or taken the risk. Every movement needs pioneers to show the way. Once the eastern entrepreneurs saw the first western microbreweries, they knew they would work back home.

I spent the years of 1985 until 1993 visiting western breweries while living on the East Coast, near Washington, D.C. I had observed the eastern microbreweries open since the first days of Weeping Radish in North Carolina, Stoudt in Pennsylvania, Dock Street in Philadelphia, Olde Heurich in Washington, William Newman's in Albany, New Amsterdam in New York, Commonwealth and Boston Beer in Boston, and Geary's in Maine. All were included in my first book, *Star Spangled Beer,* which was published in 1987.

The eastern microbreweries were opening in the late 1980s, but at a slower pace. They seemed about five years behind the trend in the West. In actuality, the early western breweries went through their own incubation period of about five years, after the first generation appeared. But the western breweries had the advantage of being in a region that was tolerant of new cultural and business experiences.

By 1990, the microbrewing renaissance was becoming a genuine national revolution. I kept my eye on the eastern microbreweries and observed that they were reaching a critical mass in New England and the mid-Atlantic states. It was time to write about them as their own regional story. And what a story it is.

To write this book, I visited craft breweries from New England to Florida over the course of several years. My research included visits to most of the breweries listed and interviews with brewers, owners, staff, consumers, and other sources. I returned three times after my move west in 1993 (see Postscript).

In addition to visits and interviews, I read widely the brewing trade press and other publications from business journals to international publications. The microbrewing movement is fortunate to have such a literate and energetic trade press with numerous brewspapers, magazines, and newsletters. My appreciation goes to the editors and publishers who help keep me informed about this very dynamic industry. They're doing first-class reporting. And their readers appreciate their hard work.

CRAFT BREWERIES VS. "MICRO" BREWERIES

I'd like to explain why I prefer to use the term "craft" breweries. The industry has matured in the last few years and has become very diversified – contract breweries, brewpubs, regional breweries, basement family breweries, and the traditional microbreweries.

The term "micro" means small production, which is not completely accurate. At one time, "micro" referred to any brewery that brewed less than 10,000 barrels a year, later changed to 15,000 barrels. I find that term limiting and misleading. It's just a number and does not indicate the maturation, growth, and sophistication in the industry.

I prefer the word "craft" breweries because it indicates how and what they brew. These brewers are artisans brewing a range of beer styles in the craft tradition – small batches, with traditional brewing ingredients, no adjuncts, and sold regionally. Craft breweries are different because of their products – not because they are small. In brewing, small is beautiful. It's also a sign of quality and diversity, which is what makes the mighty engine of American free enterprise hum. This is a craft industry, and no longer a micro industry.

WHERE – AND WHAT IS THE BIG EAST?

Another clarification – the term "Big East." The designation was coined in the early 1980s with the birth of the Big East basketball conference. The conference teams principally came from Boston, New York, Philadelphia, and Washington – part of the same areas covered in this book. Being a graduate of Georgetown University, one of the Big East schools, I like the term because it has a connotation of regional pride and distinction. The Big East means prestige, high class, talent, a quality program, and national leadership. Big East originally may have referred to a college basketball conference, but I believe it also applies to the eastern craft brewing industry. I hope you'll go along with the literary license.

Take a Big East Brewery Adventure. Visit a craft brewery, taste the delicious beers, try brewing at home, go to a beer festival, read about the eastern brewing tradition, and become a part of the Big East beer culture.

Get thee to a brewery!

ACKNOWLEDGMENTS

My appreciation goes to friends and associates living in Virginia, who have been helpful in my publishing venture. Mike Abraham of the Vienna Inn in Vienna, Joe Whitcraft in Oakton, Rolando Garces of Garces Communications in Herndon, Shirley Schulz in Herndon, and Tom Ruddy in Alexandria, have all played an important role in keeping RedBrick Press going. The editors and publishers of *Yankee Brew News, Ale Street News, Barleycorn, Southern Draft, On Tap* newsletter, and *All About Beer* magazine provided supporting research material on the region. Phil Katz at the Beer Institute in Washington, D.C., Dave Edgar at the Institute for Brewing Studies in Boulder, Colorado, supplied data on annual production. The Library Company of Philadelphia, Yuengling Brewery, Herb & Helen Haydock of the Museum of Brewing History in Ft. Mitchell, Kentucky, the New York Public Library, and Anheuser-Busch Breweries generously provided photos for the historical chapters. Rich Wagner of Hatboro, Pennsylvania, provided material on Pennsylvania's brewing heritage. And my thanks go to all the breweries who supplied information, labels, and time for interviews.

Dave Ogaz of Graphico in Sonoma, California, designed marketing material; Julia Ryan of Dunn & Associates in Hayward, Wisconsin, illustrated the cover; Janet Volkman of Sonoma, California, provided proofreading and editing service; and Joseph Maas and Shirley Foster of Paragon3 in Santa Rosa, California, provided the internal design.

Thanks to all of you for contributing your talents to the book. I enjoyed working with you.

P.S. A PERSONAL POSTSCRIPT

I moved out west in 1993 to set up my publishing company in Sonoma, California. Life is full of ironies, and the irony about the move is that Sonoma is where the first startup microbrewery, New Albion, opened in 1976. Sonoma is a quiet, semi-rural community in the wine-growing Sonoma Valley north of San Francisco. It's easy to see how it happened here.

Sonoma is a town with a long and colorful history. The flags of Spain, England, Russia, the Mexico Empire and Republic of Mexico had flown over northern California by the early 1800s. It was the location of the Mission San Francisco Solano de Sonoma, established on July 4, 1832, by Father Jose Altimira. The Sonoma Mission was the last and northernmost of the 23 missions built by the Franciscan fathers in a chain that extended from San Diego to Sonoma. On June 14, 1846, a band of Californian adventurers seized the Pueblo of Sonoma and arrested the Mexican General Mariano Guadalupe Vallejo. They declared the territory the Republic of California and raised a homemade Bear Flag, which became the official state flag. A month later, a U.S. Navy ship arrived in San Francisco Bay and an American flag was raised over the new territory for the first time

Agoston Harazsty, a Hungarian immigrant, founded the California wine industry when he planted the first vineyards in 1871, in Sonoma. Sonoma County is also home to the boutique wineries that started the California wine revolution in the 1960s. About two dozen craft breweries are within two hours drive from Sonoma. They also make great cheese and bread here. The ocean is an hour away, as is San Francisco. The location makes research more pleasant.

≋ INTRODUCTION ≋

BUILDING ON A BREWING TRADITION

America is a nation proud of its history. Although the United States has been a federal republic for a little over 200 years, we are proud of our many accomplishments in those two-plus centuries. We weren't a nation before the Revolutionary War and the Declaration of Independence, but we regard the first settlers and the colonial era as an intrinsic part of our nation's heritage. We are as patriotic about our colonial heritage as we are about our history as a sovereign nation.

Every school child learns about the Pilgrims, the first Thanksgiving, the uneasy relations with the native Americans, building a country from the forests and meadows, and the passionate radicalism that led to the Declaration of Independence, the Revolutionary War, and our Constitution.

Children also learn some of the early social history – the first settlers coming for religious freedom, immigrants coming from all European nations, and the slaves, brought from Africa and the Caribbean as a source of cheap labor. They learn how colonial farmers, some of whom became presidents and diplomats, and the tradesmen and craftsmen built a new and lasting economy with their bare hands and meager tools that has become the most powerful in the world.

One aspect of our social history that is little appreciated is the role that beer played in our nation's history. Yes, beer. A product that some perceive only as a social beverage produced at brewing factories and advertised with slick TV ads and billboards.

In reality, beer is the most American of all beverages. The Pilgrims drank it as did the sailors on the *Mayflower* who delivered them. The early settlers and colonists made beer at home or in taverns and drank it almost every day. Our Founding Fathers all drank it and many even brewed it.

When the United States entered the Industrial Revolution, breweries were one of the first industries to benefit from the new technology, cheap labor, national markets, and the economies of producing large amounts. Brewing in the Industrial Revolution became large, efficient, and very profitable.

No other beverage has the continuity of beer in our history. Beer is a historical thread from the landing of the Pilgrims to our current interdependent, international economy with global markets, corporate conglomerates, the mass media, and billions of dollars in sales. The Pilgrims and Founding Fathers may have drunk a little wine, but they certainly didn't have fruit juice, soft drinks, sports drinks, or bottled waters. They drank beer. Lots of it. And they loved it. They wrote songs and poems about beer, and served it at weddings, funerals, baptisms, ordinations, and any occasion where social intercourse took place. They drank it at taverns, in homes, in private clubs, on ships, and at farms. They drank it while they worked and where they worked. It was as commonplace as water.

Beer has a glorious and romantic history in America – almost more than any other food. And beer is a food. That argument has been substantiated in many journals that don't need to be repeated here.

COLONIAL BREWING TO CRAFT BREWING

Brewing in the 18th and 19th centuries had been prominent in Atlantic Ocean seaports. Trade and commerce developed in these ports as soon as settlers started to make a life in the New World. Boston, New York, Philadelphia, and Baltimore each had a colonial brewing tradition when all beer was ale and drunk in pub taverns where it was brewed. It was in these same Atlantic seaboard cities that the first Big East craft breweries started up.

New York's New Amsterdam contract brewery and Manhattan Brewpub started in 1984 and 1985. Boston Beer contract brewery and Commonwealth Brewpub began in Boston in 1985 and 1986. Stoudt Brewery opened in Adamstown, Pennsylvania, in 1987, as did Dock Street contract-brewing in Philadelphia. In Baltimore, Sisson's brewpub opened in 1989 near the popular Inner Harbor.

The craft brewing movement was not lost on eastern regional breweries whose history went back to the 19th century. Pennsylvania's Yuengling, The Lion, and Pittsburgh breweries and New York's F. X. Matt Brewery retooled to make craft beers under their own labels or for contract-brewing marketers. Olde Heurich, a Washington family brewery that traced its origins to the 1870s, was revived by the founder's grandson in 1986 by contracting with Pittsburgh Brewing. Mass. Bay Brewing in Boston, Geary's in Portland, Maine, and Northampton Brewpub in Northampton, Massachusetts, were part of the first wave of New England craft breweries to start up in the late 1980s.

And so it went, from Maine all the way to Florida. The craft brewing revolution came to the East Coast with a flair that made beer lovers proud of their local beers. By 1993, the East was awash in beer festivals, brewspapers, homebrewing, and beer dinners.

There has never been a better time to drink beer in the East. The Big East beer culture is alive, flourishing, and growing every day. The future promises to be one full of good beer, delightful beer festivals, entertaining beer dinners, and millions of consumers becoming educated about the history of brewing in America. Within a couple years, craft breweries will be in almost every Big East region. The East will be as well-known as a center for the brewing renaissance as any other region in the country.

Beer is no longer a commodity, but a way of life. This is a New Age, when breweries are not strictly industrial factories but brewpub restaurants and family and investor-owned craft breweries.

The craft brewing tradition started almost 400 years ago when the first colonists set foot here and began building a new life. They had beer on the ships that brought them, and they brewed it as soon as they could get supplies. They came for freedom and brought their Old World brewing traditions with them. We're a grateful nation. They brought us beer and made it a part of their lives. Now it's a part of ours.

≈ CHAPTER ONE ≈

COLONIAL BREWING –
A NATION FOUNDED ON BEER

European settlers found a hostile world when they landed in the New World in the late 16th and early 17th centuries. The months-long voyages from Europe were difficult and exhausting. The weather in the northern climates from Massachusetts to North Carolina was cold and forbidding. The land was not immediately ready for cultivation. Natives were curious but not always hospitable. And the food – what there was of it – was poor, inadequate, and of questionable nutritional value.

Food was the most precious commodity that determined if a settlement would survive. And food in the 16th and 17th centuries also meant beer. Not the yellow, gassy pilsener we're used to in the present time, but a dark, cloudy ale that was as much a food as it was an intoxicant. A ration of ale helped meet the dietary requirement for colonists in a new and dangerous place. Without adequate food and beer, no one could survive.

When the first settlers came to Virginia in 1607, a diary noted that the harsh conditions meant that "there remained neither tavern, beer house, nor place of reliefe." The first Virginia settlement backed by the London Company nearly failed because of the Starving Time of 1609–10. Only when a supply ship with provisions including beer arrived did the colony become permanent. The need for beer was of such importance that an advertisement appeared in 1609 in a London newspaper for a qualified brewer to come to Virginia to brew for the struggling colony.

The first attempts to brew in colonial Virginia proved disastrous. A brewing accident was blamed on two brother brewers, James and Jeffrey Duppa, that reputedly caused the deaths of 200 because of the "stinking Dupper beer." The shortage of drinkable beer was noted as late as 1623 by Virginia governor, Sir Francis Wyatt, who noted that there was sickness in the colony because of "want of beere, poultry, mutton, &c."

THE PILGRIMS AND THEIR BELOVED ALE

One of the most treasured anecdotes in the annals of beer lore is the role it played in the settlement of the Pilgrims in the Massachusetts colony in 1620. The captain's log aboard the *Mayflower* reported that the Pilgrims were ordered ashore so the ship could return to England because "we could not now take time for further search or consideration, our victuals being much spent, especially our Beere."[1]

This episode revealed the importance of beer in settling Massachusetts. Later efforts to colonize Massachusetts learned their lesson from the *Mayflower* experience, and ships destined for the colony carried beer for settlers and crew alike. The log on the *Arbella,* destined for a new Massachusetts colony in 1628, mentioned "42 Tonnes of Beer (about 10,000 gallons)" and "4 Pompes per water and beer (about 200 gallons)."[2]

Beer was more than something consumed for pleasure or relaxation. On sea voyages, ale was part of provisions to prevent scurvy. Although vitamin-rich citrus fruits were the preferred preventative, beer was more available and did not spoil like fruit. As any amateur brewer knows, some of the by-products of fermenting grain are vitamins and trace minerals.

A 17th-century ship captain wouldn't think of leaving port without an adequate stock of beer below deck. On voyages to the New World, beer was as important as cured meat, cooking utensils, rope for rigging, and farm tools for settlers. The logs of early settlers frequently mentioned the amount of beer carried on board and shipped to colonists. Beer kept well during travel, while water became foul in wooden barrels.

Beer was carried on ships and sold to colonists, but the supplies were limited, and early colonists seemed perpetually in need of beer. Barley and hops had to be exported from England, but the supply lines were long and the expense great. Clearing and cultivating the virgin land for crops was slow and tedious.

COLONIAL ALE –
MORE THAN JUST A GLASS OF JOY

Beer – or more accurately ale – was a far different product from what we drink today. Although it was drunk for relaxation and social purposes, its low alcohol versions of "table" or "small" beer were the beverage of the day for young and old alike. Disease and plagues had been common since the Middle Ages, and most sources of water were carriers of disease. Beer, on the other hand, was more reliable from a health standpoint because the alcohol killed mild forms of bacteria. Beer was more healthful than colonists may have known.

This fear of waterborne disease came with the colonists when they first arrived. But they were eventually forced to drink the water and were surprised at the fresh taste. "I dare not preferre it before good Beere as some have done, but any man would choose it before Bad Beere, Wheay, or Buttermilk," one hardy colonist wrote of New England water.[3]

ALE IN THE HEALTHY COLONIAL HOME

Beer and alcohol were part of the ordinary diet for everyone – men, women, children, and the elderly. It was considered healthful and soothing for the temperament. It warmed the body, promoted digestion and regularity, soothed moods, and made work easier. Those who did not partake of beer and other alcoholic beverages were considered suspect. Why, after all, would one not want to drink beer if it provided a source of nourishment, had a refreshing taste, and eased the burdens of day-to-day life?

Brewing beer for home and tavern consumption was commonplace in the colonies by the 1670s. Brewing at home likely began as soon as baggage and tools were removed from the ships and dwellings constructed. A few small commercial breweries did start up, but by far the most common source of beer was the domestic operation, usually managed by the wife or women in the family. Brewing was as much a part of family life as baking bread, cooking, and preserving. The utensils were even the same – spoons, kettles, and barrels. Brewing was most likely scheduled routinely with other kitchen chores to guarantee an adequate supply for the family. The style was similar to a dark ale or our modern-day porter.

Colonists depended upon England for their supply of malted barley and hops. Newly cultivated farmland was more profitably used for growing tobacco, a popular commodity for trade with the Old World. Those who could not afford expensive imported English malting barley resorted to brewing with molasses,  corn, maize, or even pumpkins. Mugs of ale were on colonial tables whenever food was served, morning to night. The day began with a few mugs of breakfast ale. It was how the body received nourishment in the morning before undertaking daily, arduous chores. Vitamin-rich foods, fruits, and vegetables were not plentiful, but beer was easier to come by.

And since beer provided important daily dietary needs, the task of brewing was important for survival. It wasn't just beer, it was food to live by. Without beer, life would have been more harsh.

Beer was not the only alcoholic beverage enjoyed by colonists. Following customs in the Old World, they drank alcoholic and non-alcoholic drinks concocted from many ingredients and recipes. In addition to traditional beer, wine, rum, and brandy, colonists consumed mead (beer brewed with honey), metheglin (ale made with balme, mint, fennel, rosemary, thyme, and other spices), tea, chocolate, sage tea, mumm (ale with oat or wheat malt added), cider, sillabub (cider, sugar, cream, and nutmeg stirred but not boiled), aqua-vitae, claret, beverige (a sweet drink made with water, sugar, cider and spices), switchel (similar to beverige but fortified with vinegar and rum), ebulum (made from ale and the juices of elder or juniper berries and spices), sack, perry (fermented pear juice), peachy (fermented peach juice), flip (beer sweetened with sugar or molasses, dried pumpkin, and rum and stirred with a hot poker), canary (wine), punch, and sack-possett (ale and sack).

SOCIAL IMPACT OF COLONIAL BREWING

The problems of drinking were evident in the colonies as it was in every society. Drunkenness was a concern, because communities and village life was so interdependent. If conduct did not promote harmony, the colony itself would be endangered. But the colonists usually had more to worry about than social drinking. Almost everyone drank alcohol and enjoyed its benefits.

Various institutions had a strong effect on personal conduct: families, the church, and friends were always there to guard against excesses. Drunkenness was considered a personal problem, and not a deep social ill requiring anything more than a few restrictions or admonitions for the guilty to get right. But there was no effort to promote a total prohibition of drinking – it was just too much a part of life for everyone.

Social conduct was monitored by legal means. Colonial taverns were licensed by the local authorities, and codes of conduct were posted to show what taverns could serve, when, and at what cost. Civic authorities levied penalties for drunkenness, and churches made drunkards pay for their redemption. Social harmony was promoted for obvious reasons – survival and public welfare.

Already by 1634, the price of beer was regulated by colonial authorities. The price of a meal was sixpence, while a quart of ale was a penny. A tavern owner who charged more could be fined 10 shillings for gouging patrons. The drinker, on the other hand, could also be fined if he drank more than a quart at a meal. This was to avoid the habit of "bye-drinking" – quaffing a few mugs of beer and chatting with friends into the late hours.

The Puritans in Massachusetts were active in monitoring social behavior. By 1636, Puritan authorities had passed measures to fine and imprison those who drank too much or tavern keepers who overserved their customers. All of New England was under the influence of monitoring of social activities such as drinking. The result was a community on guard against excess or unhealthy behavior. The clergy and other self-appointed officials were only too happy to set standards and then enjoy enforcing them. Drinking didn't diminish, it just was kept within boundaries of "community acceptance."

COLONIAL TAVERN LIFE

Taverns were one of the most important cultural institutions in American colonial life. All villages and towns had pubs or taverns for socializing, eating, and providing lodging for travelers. Most were licensed and brewed their own ale. All during the day, colonists would stop by the local taverns to exchange gossip, spread the news, enjoy a good meal and drink, and spend time with friends, neighbors, and family. They were the hub of social life in the colonies.

With such an important role to play, there was always a fair amount of politicking going on in colonial taverns. It was where one went to find out what the clergy or civic leaders were proposing, when funerals, weddings, or holiday celebrations were scheduled, and to meet new arrivals in the village. Social gatherings at taverns would go on for hours, often in front of a roaring fireplace with many pints of ale downed during the evening. The tavern also served a practical use as a place for the local militia to rally. The reason was simple – everyone knew where taverns were, and they could be a source of food, drink, and lodging, if the militia needed them.

Colonial innkeepers were established and well-respected members of the community. Before politicians became representatives of the community, inn or tavern keepers filled the role quite adequately. They were reliable and visible members of the community and oftentimes the most prominent citizens. Taverns were a vital part of early American life – faithfully patronized and well regarded by colonists. Those who did not gather and drink at local taverns were thought to be eccentric or stuffy. Mealtime was accompanied by beer or cider at home and drafts at tavern. By modern standards, everyone was a moderate or heavy drinker. Every person above the age of 15 years old drank six gallons of alcohol each year, or about 34 gallons of beer. Much of this was the low-alcohol "small" or "table" beer, but it is more than the current average for adults.

The first law permitting brewpubs – taverns where beer could be brewed and sold – was passed in Massachusetts in 1638. This might have been because civic leaders wanted to promote consumption of beer instead of spirits, which were seen as destructive to common order and lawfulness. Beer was the alcohol beverage preferred by many in the early 17th century who feared the ill effects of cheap rum and whiskey which lead to intemperate ways.

The social importance of taverns was not lost on the local political authorities. In order to keep them orderly, local officials regulated taverns to insure that only proprietors of the highest order would run them and conduct business in a responsible manner. Similar laws were passed in the Virginia colonies. A history of the Virginia colony published in 1629 already mentioned two brewhouses: "For drink, some malt the Indian corne, others barley, of which they make good Ale, both strong and small, and such plentie thereof, few of the upper Planters drink any water, but the better sort are well furnished with Sacke, Aquavitae, and good English Beere."[4] In 1649, a pamphlet published in London described the appealing life in Virginia, praising the good barley and hops, the six "publick brewhouses and most brew their own beer, strong and good. ...Men are provided with all necessaries, have plenty of victual, bread, and good beer, and housing, all which the Englishman loves full dearly."[5]

Colonists drank ale from tankards or mugs made of pewter, leather, stoneware, or wood. The well-to-do would show their affluence by using silver tankards. Paul Revere was a Massachusetts silversmith and likely made drinking tankards for his clientele. Glass, although it was manufactured by colonial craftsmen, was not widely used for drinking purposes before the 18th century. More common drinking receptacles were heavy black leather mugs known as "black Jacks," that were waxed, bound, and trimmed with silver.

EARLY COMMERCIAL COLONIAL BREWERIES – NEW NETHERLANDS 1630-64

Early colonization of the New World was largely accomplished by the English and Dutch. Both were eager to bring quality brewing to their fellow countrymen as a way of providing traditional social customs into their colonies. The year after the Pilgrims landed in Massachusetts, the Dutch established the West India Company to colonize the Hudson River and Mohawk Valley, where Dutch fur trappers had been exploiting the rich resources of the region. The first two Dutch colonies were at Fort Orange (present-day Albany) and Fort Nassau (Camden, New Jersey).

The Dutch used the "patroon" system, whereby the government gave land grants to those willing to absorb the cost of settlement. As a result, Dutch colonies were settled by those with the wealth to support the transporting and provisioning of settlers. One of the first patroons was Kiliaen van Rensselaier, an Amsterdam jeweler, who was granted land on the Hudson River near Fort Orange. Although he never visited his new land, he wrote in his journal that as soon as grain could be grown, he intended to build a brewery to provide New Netherlands with beer. The brewery existed in Albany sometime around 1637.

Peter Minuit arrived at Manhattan and bought the island from the natives naming it New Amsterdam. The Dutch built a fort and trading post at the southern tip for security and trading between inland trappers and ships arriving from the Old World. One of New Amsterdam's first buildings was a brewery built in 1632 not far from the fort. The brewery was located on a road later named "Brouwers (Brewers) Street" for the breweries that were built there.

New Amsterdam's seaport became a destination for foreign sailors, craftsmen, tradesmen, trappers, and farmers. A popular gathering place was the White Horse Tavern, near the present-day Battery, which consisted of a single room measuring approximately 18 x 25 feet. Despite its modest size, the White Horse Tavern was a lively place. One account said: "It was always crowded with drinkers during the legal drinking hours, which were from early morning until ten in the evening, and did a brisk business after hours as well as during church service on Sunday, when drinking was also banned." [6]

The West India Company was also in the business of operating taverns. In 1642, the director of the company (more like a mayor), erected a stone inn called the City Tavern (Stadt Herberg) so he would not have to be the host for visiting officials and traders in his own home. The City Tavern eventually became the City Hall (Stadt Huys) where New Amsterdam's first political meetings were held. One of the official duties of assemblymen who gathered there was to regulate the tavern and brewing trades.

A survey of New Amsterdam in 1638 revealed that one-fourth of the buildings were licensed to sell beer and tobacco –17 licensed taverns and 7 homebrew markets. The early records of New Amsterdam indicated that the sale of most houses included the transfer of the separate brewhouses. Many of New Amsterdam's first commercial brewers became wealthy and influential–Jacob Kip, William Beekman, Oloff van Cortlandt, and the three Bayard brothers who were nephews of Peter Stuyvesant.

New Amsterdam was home to some 10 breweries by 1650. The first colonial brewery established under its own name was the Red Lion Brewery operated by Isaac de Forest. The Red Lion operated from 1660–75 and was mentioned in numerous journals by Dutch settlers, who said it brewed beer as good as that brewed back in the Netherlands. One of the Red Lion's accounts was the Dutch Reformed church, which bought beer for serving at funerals. The Dutch never seemed to lack for good beer in the colonies.

The Dutch regulated commercial breweries and required them to be licensed and pay taxes. These breweries were operated by private companies, patroons, tavern keepers, and individual colonists. The busy brewing by the Dutch was no doubt influenced by the wild hops found growing in New Netherlands and the Dutch farmers who planted rye, barley, wheat, oats, and hops for brewing strong beer. After the Revolutionary War, New York State was a center for hop growing until the 1850s.

BREWING IN 18TH-CENTURY PHILADELPHIA

Philadelphia became the first colonial town known as a center for brewing. It had all the advantages that made it an important center for commerce and trade–location on a river and outlet to the sea, halfway between the Massachusetts and southern colonies, and a busy seaport for trade among the colonies and the New World. Philadelphia's first recorded brewery was established early in the town's history in 1683 by William Frampton on Front Street between Walnut and Spruce Streets.

Pennsylvania's most celebrated personality in early colonial days was William Penn, an English Quaker. Penn had received a land grant in 1680 from Charles II to establish a colony for Quakers. He built his own manor house in Pennsbury, 20 miles north of Philadelphia. Penn loved beer and had a brewhouse constructed at Pennsbury which lasted for almost 200 years. During the little time Penn spent in Pennsylvania, he entertained the governors of Maryland and Virginia, visiting dignitaries, and Indians at Pennsbury. Penn believed that Indians deserved property rights and granted a Great Treaty with them in 1683.

Another Quaker family, the Morrises, were Philadelphia's most famous brewers during the city's first century. In 1687, Anthony Morris built the city's second brewery on Front Street near Frampton's brewery on the

Delaware River. Morris became Philadelphia's second mayor in 1703 and was elected Supreme Judge of the Commonwealth in 1705. Morris is depicted in Benjamin West's painting "Penn's Treaty with the Indians," where he is shown wearing Quaker dress.

Morris died in 1721, and the family brewery passed to his son, Anthony Morris II. In 1741, Morris turned half of the brewery over to his son, Anthony Morris III, who later brought his two sons, Anthony Morris IV and Thomas, into the business. Anthony Morris IV was killed during the Revolutionary War at the Battle of Princeton. Thomas became a prominent civic leader who built the Philadelphia Library, a Quaker school, was manager of the Pennsylvania Hospital, and owned an insurance business. He died in 1809.

Another well-known Philadelphian brewer was Quaker George Emlen who owned a brewery on Fifth Street above Chestnut. Emlen's father had arrived in Philadelphia in 1682 and built a brewery that became quite profitable. Emlen became wealthy and built a mansion in Whitemarsh Township, 12 miles from Philadelphia. In November 1777, George Washington used Emlen's mansion as his Colonial Army Headquarters before he moved his troops on to Valley Forge for the winter.

Philadelphian Ben Franklin loved his beer so much he had an account with a brewery in 1736, according to his personal papers. Franklin's landlord, Timothy Matlack, was a brewer whose brewhouse and malthouse were on Market Street. Matlack moved out of his home in 1750, and Franklin and his wife, Deborah, leased the home. A subsequent owner of Matlack's brewery lead a procession of Philadelphia's brewers in a 1788 parade commemorating the signing of the Declaration of Independence and ratification of the proposed Constitution.

Philadelphia breweries developed such a following that their beers were exported to other colonies, principally in the south where beer was scarce. The City of Brotherly Love even became known for its own style of beer. According to one of the recipes, Philadelphia beer was made with molasses or treacle and had raisins added before being put into bottles or barrels. A brewery in San Francisco in the late 1800s was called the Philadelphia Brewery.

George Washington was not the only lover of a good pint among the Founding Fathers. Washington's favorite beer was porter brewed by Robert Hare's brewery in Philadelphia. Hare had emigrated from England to Philadelphia in 1773 with money his father had given him to start a brewery. Hare possibly brewed the first porter in America.

Washington ordered his porter from Hare's brewery through an importer, Clement Biddle. Hare was so busy brewing porter that he had to rely on importers or distributors to sell his beer. When Washington was serving as the nation's first President and living in New York, he instructed his secretary, Tobias Lear: "Will you be so good as to desire Mr. Hare to have if he continues to make the best Porter in Philadlephia 3 gross of his best put up for Mount Vernon? as the President means to visit that place in the recess of Congress and it is probable there will be a large demand for Porter at that time." [7]

Unfortunately, Hare's brewery burned in 1790, and Washington wrote from Mount Vernon of the great loss: "on public as well as private accts., to hear of Mr. Hares loss." He instructed Lear, "you wd. do well to lay in a pretty good Stock of his, or some other Porter." [8]

When Washington made plans to leave office and move to Mount Vernon, he again wrote to have porter shipped to his home for his drinking and entertaining. The porter came from the brewery owned by Benjamin Morris, a descendant of Anthony Morris, whose brewery, built in 1745, was most likely at the corner of Dock and Pear Streets.

NEW ENGLAND BREWING

From the earliest days of Harvard College, founded in 1636, beer was provided to students at daily meals. Enrollment at Harvard was less than 100 students, who relied upon the university for their board. A brewhouse was erected on the Cambridge campus which made both single (small) and double (strong) beer. More than one brewhouse was recorded in Harvard's records; two were destroyed by fire. Beer was also part of the "tuition" paid by students. Wheat or malt was taken in trade, which was not uncommon. Harvard's students and administration alike regarded beer as an important part of the university's responsibilities. The first president of Harvard, Nathaniel Eaton, was dismissed because he could not reliably provide beer for students, a job which usually fell to the wife in the family.

Two of Boston's earliest commercial breweries were started by John Carey and John Williams. Carey received permission to build a 50 ft. long brewhouse on Cambridge Street in 1710, and Williams received permission to build a brewery in 1716. Sampson Salter was another early Boston brewer who supplied beer to ships in Boston harbor owned by Peter Faneuil. Boston's small commercial breweries found steady business by serving the ships anchored in Boston harbor.

The Adamses were one of colonial Boston's most famous families, but their profession was malting, not brewing. The Adams family malting house had been started in Braintree in 1694 by Joseph, great-grandfather of the patriot Samuel, Jr. Samuel Adams, Sr., died in 1748 and gave the malthouse to his son, Samuel, Jr., who was born in 1722. Samuel Adams, Jr., worked in the malthouse next to the family home on Purchase Street but apparently never had a liking for business. He sold the family malthouse in 1763 to change careers and spread revolution in the colonies.

SOUTHERN COLONIES

Brewing never fully developed in the colonies south of Virginia, mainly for geographic and climatic reasons. The hot, humid weather and sandy soils were not hospitable for growing barley or hops. Southern plantations tried to grow hops, but the experiment failed. As a result, beer for the southern colonies was imported from the north or from England. Efforts were made to brew locally, the most notable examples being in Virginia and Maryland. Maryland's first brewery was built in Baltimore in 1794.

Virginia was already well developed and prosperous by the 1700s. One of the colony's first institutions was William and Mary College, in Williamsburg, founded in 1693. William and Mary, like Boston's Harvard, had its own brewery. The brewery was located in the quadrangle where baking, brewing, and cooking were done and receptions held for university officials and scholars. When the college's brewery burned down, it was hastily rebuilt. The Governor's House in Williamsburg also had its own brewhouse, no doubt to provide the governor with a constant supply of freshly brewed ale.

Alexandria, Virginia, on the Potomac River north of George Washington's home in Mt. Vernon, was the home of several breweries in the late 18th century. The Wales Brewery (1771–1802), Potowmack Brewery (c.1793–1807), and Union brewery (1794–1821?) all were operating before the nation's capital was built across the river. The Wales and

Potowmack breweries were located in warehouses on the Potomac River. Washington's Mt. Vernon home south of the city was a 15-mile carriage ride away, and Washington probably visited the breweries to purchase their wares. His family church was Christ Church in the center of Alexandria and less than a half mile from the Potomac River.

An early commercial brewery was established in Fredericksburg, Virginia, in 1771, but it was apparently a failure. It was put up for auction, but no buyers were willing to take it over. All the property, including the slave cooper, were sold. Slaves in the southern colonies, particularly women, learned brewing in addition to their regular chores of washing, ironing, sewing, and baking.

Despite the number of family, tavern, and small commercial breweries, most of Virginia's beer came from New York, Philadelphia, and England.

James Oglethorpe wanted to prohibit the sale or consumption of spirits in the Georgia colony, but encouraged importing strong beer and molasses from England. This prohibition led to smuggling and bootlegging rum until the ban was lifted. Oglethorpe knew the desire for beer. When taking a boat trip in 1736, he put the "strong beer" on the fastest boat to encourage lazy boaters who might dally along during the day. If they didn't keep up with the lead boat by nightfall, they'd have to bed down without their nightly ration of beer.

ALE AND REVOLUTION

Ale was such a common commodity in the colonies that it is no surprise that it got mixed up in revolutionary politics. Nowhere was politics more hotly debated than in the popular taverns. It was in taverns that the King and his taxes were condemned, the British Army ridiculed, and the fever of independence fueled. The British felt taverns were the dens of

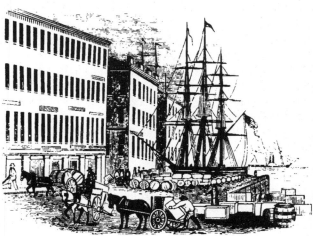

sedition and tyranny; revolutionaries embraced them as hothouses for independence. What better way to pass the time of day than by downing a few pints and debating the revolutionary issue of the day.

Beer also became embroiled

in revolutionary disputes between the Crown and colonial merchants. In the 1760s, colonists had agreed to boycott malt from England to protest taxes levied by George III to pay for the end of the Seven Years War against France. A test of the colonists' resolve came in 1769 when a shipment of malt from Yarmouth arrived in Philadelphia aboard the *Charming Polly*. The English wanted to tempt the colonists to recant their boycott and admit their dependence on England for brewers' malt. The malt was for delivery to Amos Trettell, a maltster who had not ordered it. But word of the malt's arrival quickly spread around the city.

Philadelphia merchants called a meeting to discuss the malt shipment and to strengthen the resolve of city residents. Philadelphia brewers lobbied to boycott the malt, arguing that if beer could be brewed in the city, there was no need to have the English product. A vote was held and the boycott was confirmed. A few days later, the *Charming Polly* sailed away with its cargo of malt intact. A blow for brewing independence had been struck!

BEER RATIONS DURING WAR

When the Revolutionary War started, the Colonial Army was less than prepared despite the prior agitation and hostilities. From the formation of the army under the command of George Washington in November 1775, provisions for beer were included in military supply orders. Each soldier in the Continental Army was to receive "1 part of spruce beer or cyder per man per day."[9] Beer was preferred by commanders instead of the more potent rum, whisky, or brandy, which might make the troops unmanageable. The price of small beer was dropped to a shilling a quart, instead of the old price of a shilling ten pence. During the tense days leading up to the Revolutionary War, the supply of beer and food was short on both English and colonial sides. Abigail Adams wrote to her husband, John, in Philadelphia, that the supply of beer, malt, and cider was gone. The supply of beer was so short that the British commander ordered London brewers to ship 500 butts of strong beer to his troops in Boston.

While Washington was in the vicinity of New York in the spring of 1776, his troop's beer rations were supplied by William Faulkner's brewery in "Brookland Ferry." Faulkner's invoice, dated April 17, 1776, recorded an order for beer, ale, and "ship beer" sold to quartermaster General Joseph Trumbull. The invoice reads: "To 3Bbl beer for use of General Washington's Guards."[10] Washington's troops consumed some 300 barrels a day.

Regardless of his political persuasion, Faulkner was a businessman. After Washington moved his army north to Valley Forge, British troops moved into the area. Faulkner saw the opportunity and gained a contract to supply British troops in New York. Faulkner no doubt believed that lovers of ale had no allegiance. Thirsty troops were thirsty troops and needed to be accommodated. Faulkner wasn't the first or last brewer to recognize that business is business. Solvency rules.

COLONIAL BEER RECIPES

The quality of beer in the colonies was often inconsistent due to the supply of barley and hops. And when revolutionary storm clouds were gathering in the 1760s, brewers were eager to find alternatives to imported malt. On February 14, 1775, the *Virginia Gazette* published a recipe to make beer from green corn stalks. The stalks were chopped, boiled to extract the juice, which was boiled as in a normal mashing, and hops were added. This was, in fact, George Washington's recipe for "small beer" which he wrote in a notebook when he was in the Virginia militia. Today is in the New York Public Library.

Brewers, as do cooks, like nothing more than trying new recipes. When conventional brewing supplies were low, brewers experimented with coriander, ginger, and cinnamon. Other herbs used in brewing were Alexandria, senna, "Hock," and fabia amora. Spruce beer was a favorite of Benjamin Franklin, who brought back his own recipe from France after the Revolution when he was ambassador. Pumpkin, apples, and peaches were fermented to make flavored beers. Molasses was often included in colonial recipes; the sweet syrup was similar to modern-day malt extract used in home brewing.

One writer from the 1630s referenced this ingenuity in finding substitutes for barley and hops:

> *If barley be wanting to make into malt*
> *We must be content and think it no fault*
> *For we can make liquor to sweeten our lips*
> *of pumpkins, and parsnips, and walnut-tree chips.*[11]

(Opposite Page)

GEORGE WASHINGTON'S HOME BREW RECIPE
WRITTEN WHEN HE WAS IN THE VIRGINIA MILITIA
To Make Small Beer
Take a large Siffer full of Bran Hops to your taste–Boil these 3 hours. Then strain out 30 Gall (n) into a Cooler put in 3 Gall (n) Molasses while the Beer is Scalding hot or rather draw the Molasses into the Cooler. Strain the Beer on it while boiling Hot. let this stand till it is little more than Blood Warm then put in a quart of Ye (a) st if the weather is very cold cover it over with a Blank (et) let it work in the Cooler 24 hours then put it into the Cask–leave the Bung open till it is almost done working–Bottle it that day Week it was Brewed.
(Reprinted with permission. New York Public Library)

To make Small Beer -

Take a large Sifter full of Bran
Hops to your taste - Boil these
3 hours. then strain out 30 Gall.
into a Cooler put in 3 Gall.
Molasses while the Beer is
Scalding hot, or rather draw the
Melasses into the Cooler & Strain
the Beer on it while boiling Hot
let this stand till it is little more
than Blood warm then put in
a quart of Yeast if the weather is
very Cold cover it over with a Blanket
& let it work in the Cooler 24 hours
then put it into the Cask - leave
the Bung open till it is almost don
Working - Bottle it that day week
it was Brewed

BEER VERSUS SPIRITS

After the Revolutionary War, social and economic changes came to the new nation as it approached the new century. Part of the changes had to do with Americans trying to assert their independence from the many finished goods and food commodities that had kept the colonies tied to England. Trade with all countries, however, was increasing as America's economy grew.

One of America's new trading regions in the 18th century was the West Indies. Slaves, molasses, and rum were brought into the American colonies from the West Indies. The molasses and rum were directly competitive with the brewing enterprises. Even before the Revolutionary War, consumption of distilled spirits—rum, whiskey, brandy, and gin were becoming widespread, partly because of the cost. American consumption habits changed from drinking lower alcohol beer (4–6%) to distilled spirits whose alcohol content was nearly ten times as great (45% alcohol or 90 proof). Per capita consumption of distilled spirits was nearly 4 gallons per year by 1830.[12]

The clergy, civic officials, and the medical community were concerned about drunkenness from heavy spirit consumption, treating it as a threat to sobriety and social harmony. The social impact of the excessive consumption of spirits was not lost on the new government that came to power with the ratification of the Constitution and the election of the new Congress. The first Secretary of Treasury, Alexander Hamilton, even proposed the establishment of a national brewery to encourage beer consumption. Other inducements, including favorable tax exceptions for breweries and a tax on English beer, were legislated.

Spirits consumption began to have a negative impact on brewing and the consumption of beer. State legislatures passed ordinances promoting brewing and consumption of beer as good for the community. Farm brewing was also encouraged, and farmers' publications included directions for setting up home brewing operations and obtaining beer at a fraction of the cost of commercially brewed beer. One problem was the continuing shortage of brewing malt. Imported malt might be available, but it was discouraged by those trying to cut trade ties with England. Both domestic malt and hops were available for commercial brewing, but supplies were not adequate to cover the demand for home and tavern brewing.

EARLY TEMPERANCE

The concern about spirits so alarmed Philadelphia physician Benjamin Rush that he began writing pamphlets combining medical literature with temperance propaganda. He wrote a pamphlet in 1772 urging moderate drinking, diet, and exercise. But his 1784 essay, *An Inquiry into the Effects of Spirituous Liquors,* became a *cause célèbre.*

Rush's well-reasoned argument and medical information alerted the medical community, which had ignored the spirits issue and its perceived effects on society. Rush's positions were adopted by medical schools and clergy as sound reasoning against spirits in a healthful society. Thousands of copies were printed and sent to Europe.

Rush also published a *Moral and Physical Thermometer* that connected consumption of alcoholic beverages to conduct, behavior, and health. Rush's thermometer illustrated the preferred connection between consumption of water, milk, and small beer with good health, wealth and happiness. At the bottom of his chart, Rush postulated that drinkers of punch, gin, brandy, rum, and whiskey were doomed to a life of disease, suicide, death, and imprisonment.

The issue of social conduct and drinking was beginning to have an impact on the activities of religious, political, and medical groups who felt responsible for monitoring society's behavior. Out of this concern, a temperance movement was organizing to influence the laws on making and consuming alcohol. Although it was another century before the temperance movement became a national political force, the attitudes toward alcohol were turning. The young nation was learning one of the benefits a true democracy provided – a forum for the exchange of all views in a free society.

A BREWING REVOLUTION COMES TO AMERICA

The years 1800 to 1830 were a time of wandering in the brewing community. Tavern and commercial breweries were still operating, but consumption of rum and whiskey was increasing. In Europe, another revolution was happening. Political and social unrest was bringing thousands of new immigrants to America's shores. These immigrants were fleeing the tyranny, poverty, and despair of Europe and seeking a new start in a young nation offering liberty and opportunity.

A large number of immigrants came from Germany, fleeing political repression. Many of these German immigrants had a background in brewing in local and farm breweries. Hoping to put these skills to use in their new homes, they brought the tradition and skills of an industry that had been brewing for centuries.

The German immigrants in the mid-1800s brought over tales of a new type of beer being brewed – a lighter, golden lager beer stored in cold temperatures for several weeks or months. The lager was more than a new beer – it was a revolutionary product. A few German immigrants arrived with small vials of new yeast for brewing lager. This yeast was the seeds of a brewing revolution. Just as the English and Dutch colonists had brought contemporary brewing traditions with them in the 1600s, so did the Germans in the 1800s.

YUENGLING BREWERY, THE OLDEST BREWERY IN AMERICA

The oldest brewery in America was originally founded in 1829 in Pottsville, Pennsylvania as the D.G. Yuengling Eagle Brewery by David Yuengling, a German immigrant. The Eagle brewery was one of hundreds started in Pennsylvania in the 19th century as community breweries. The original brewery was destroyed in a fire in 1831 and rebuilt on its present site on Mahantongo Street. The site was chosen because it backed into a mountain where caves were dug to store the beer at cold temperatures. Ale and porter were brewed in the early days and lager was added when yeast from Germany was brought into the country in the 1840-50s. The Yuengling Brewery today is part of the revival of the craft brewing revolution and brews several styles – ale, porter, black & tan – that had almost disappeared from America after Prohibition. (*Reprinted with permission. Yeungling Brewery*)

   The era of brewing in small commercial, farm, and home breweries was coming to an end. Science and technology were bringing dramatic changes to manufacturing. Brewing was about to become an industrial process – beer made in factories. The quaint world of cottage brewing was about to be replaced with giant factories producing thousands of barrels of a new beer.

CHAPTER ONE FOOTNOTES

1. Baron, Stanley. *Brewed in America: A History of Beer and Ale in the United States,* Little Brown, & Co., Boston, 1962, p. 7.
2. *Ibid.,* p. 9.
3. *Ibid.*
4. *Ibid.,* p. 12.
5. *Ibid.,* p. 13.
6. *Ibid.,* p 22.
7. *Ibid.,* p. 116
8. *Ibid.*
9. *Ibid.,* p. 101
10. *Ibid.,* p. 106
11. Earle, Alice Morse. *Customs and Fashions in Old New England,* Charles E. Tuttle, Rutland, Vermont, 1973. p. 174.
12. Rorabaugh, W. J. *The Alcoholic Republic: An American Tradition.* Oxford University Press, New York, 1979. p. 10.

≈ CHAPTER TWO ≈

BREWING BECOMES AN INDUSTRY

The 19th century in America was a time of great change. As the nation entered the century, John Adams was President, the first to live in the White House in Washington. The nation consisted of a handful of states on the eastern coastline with the unexplored forests and wilderness areas to the West. During the 19th century, the United States grew to a nation of more than 40 million stretching across the continent to the Pacific Ocean. Populating this vast territory were millions of new Americans who had immigrated from Europe, Africa, and Asia.

The population of colonial America, even after 150 years of settlement, was a meager 2 million. The population grew only slightly until the end of the War of 1812, when the first wave of immigrants began arriving. From 1815 until the eve of our entry into World War I a century later, 30 million immigrants arrived from Europe.

Word of the promise of America spread around the world into every tiny village, remote valley, and impoverished hut. Immigrants came to escape political repression, forced military conscription, hunger, and crushing poverty. They came with the hope of a job, religious and political freedom, and the chance for an education for their children. Their dream was a chance to improve their lives for themselves and their families.

Two nations that sent millions to America in the first waves were Ireland and Germany. In the decades of the 1840–50s, 2 million Irish fled their homeland because of the potato famine. More than 1.5 million German immigrants fled because of the revolutions of 1830 and 1848. German immigrants came as peasants, farmers, craftsmen, and political refugees and flocked to the industrial cities, where other Germans had settled. Some German immigrant farmers looked for employment on farms, but large numbers congregated in German-speaking neighborhoods in Philadelphia, New York, Brooklyn, Boston, Pittsburgh, Chicago, Cincinnati, Milwaukee, and St. Louis, where the jobs were.

THE UNITED STATES ENTERS THE INDUSTRIAL ERA

One of the most profound changes taking place in the 19th century was how the nation worked. It didn't toil on small farms and sell products at local markets, it worked in industrial cities with new immigrants who spoke Italian, German, Chinese, Greek, and Gallic. The nation evolved from an economy based upon craftsmen, merchants, and farmers into a national powerhouse with enormous factory assembly lines, crowded and polluted cities, and a nationwide railroad network. The economy also supported an expensive military force bloodied by a tragic civil war, atrocities committed against native Americans, and a few foreign entanglements. An infant democracy became an international economic giant in the 1800s.

Its culinary tastes also changed. Immigrants brought new foods and cuisines. Americans also drank a different beer. It wasn't the same old dark, muddy ale, but a clear golden lager created in a laboratory and chilled in a cellar. A beer born of science, not in a tavern or kitchen. The 19th-century industrial revolution moved brewing from the home, farm, and tavern into an urban factory.

The reason for this dramatic change was a microscopic organism that fermented sugared water into beer. Lager yeast is different from the yeast that brews ales. It thrives at colder temperatures and falls to the bottom of the vessel, hence the term, "bottom-fermented" lager. Lager yeast was cultivated in European laboratories and first brought from an unknown German brewery in the 1840s. One record indicates that this could not have happened until the Baltimore clipper ships reduced the sailing time from Europe to America to three weeks.

A Philadelphia brewer, John Wagner, obtained lager yeast in 1840 from a Bavarian brewery where he had previously worked. Wagner's crude brewery was in his home on St. John Street. He treated his German friends to this new beer and one of his friends, Charles Wolf, took a yeast sample back to his brewery downtown on Second and New Streets.

Wolf later shared the yeast with another German brewer, Charles Engle, and the two Germans built a brewery on Dillwyn Street. The Engel & Wolf brewery was for many years the resort of the Germans in Philadelphia, who more than once drank the brewery dry. Often they were compelled to display the placard that beer would again be dispensed after a certain date.[1]

ENGEL & WOLF
THE FIRST COMMERCIAL LAGER BREWERY IN AMERICA

Lager yeast from Bavaria began arriving in the United States carried over on the speedy Baltimore clipper ships. The fast passage would allow the yeast to stay alive until it arrived and was put to work in American breweries. The first commercial lager brewery was the Engel & Wolf brewery established in 1844 at 352–354 Dillwyn Street in Philadelphia. Engel & Wolf's lager was so popular with German immigrants that the brewery ran dry several times. This illustration shows beer being transported out of the caves, and passengers traveling on early steam engine railroads. *(Reprinted with permission. Library Company of Philadelphia)*

"At this locality, the first vaults suitable for the storage of lager beer were completed in 1845. With the steady influx of Germans, the business grew, and additional cellars were rented under the buildings of the Mitchell grindstone works, at York Avenue and Wood Street. Annual sales at this time were approximately 3,500 barrels."[2]

Wherever Germans gathered, they reproduced their social customs and traditions. They published German-language newspapers, organized fraternal societies, built and supported Lutheran and Catholic churches, and socialized in brewery beer gardens. Some of these beer gardens could accommodate several hundred guests, certainly an incentive to the breweries building them. These beer gardens were a bit of life back home – singing German songs, meeting friends, exchanging political news and gossip, and drinking lager beer by the hour.

LAGER BEGINS TO REPLACE ALE IN POPULARITY

It took about two decades for the popularity of lager to reach the larger market outside the immigrant community. Ale, porter, and stout were still the preferred styles until the Civil War. Even after the war, ale brewers were prospering throughout the East. In Pittsburgh, where German immigrants were numerous, the three largest breweries, Wainwright, Pittsburgh, and Shiras were all brewing ale in the 1870s. But lager was developing a following by the mid-1850s. Breweries in Philadelphia in 1858 brewed 180,000 barrels of lager, and 170,000 of ale, porter, and stout.[3]

The importation of lager yeast coincided with the industrialization of America and the move from rural areas to the cities. This evolution was reflected in breweries' growth. In 1850, there were 431 breweries in the country brewing 750,000 barrels of beer. Ten years later, there were 1,269 breweries producing more than a million barrels a year. New York and Philadelphia were still the leading brewing cities, making 85% of the beer in the country, and exporting much of it to other states.[4]

THE BREWING GIANTS

The 1850s was the decade when a number of breweries were started by German immigrants that became giants in the next century. Joseph Schlitz opened a brewery in Milwaukee in 1856. In 1851, Valentin Blatz bought the Milwaukee City Brewery and increased production. In 1855, Frederick Miller bought another Milwaukee brewery, the Plank Road Brewery, established in 1848.

In St. Louis, a soap manufacturer, Eberhard Anheuser, took over a brewery in 1857 from a small brewer named Schneider. He hired his son-in-law, Adolphus Busch, who worked for a brewers' supplier, to come to work for him. Their creation became the world's largest brewery.

This pattern of young German immigrants starting breweries was carried out all throughout America. Brooklyn, Albany, Cincinnati, Cleveland, New York, and Baltimore also had large populations of German immigrants who started breweries.

BREWERY TAXES FUND WARS

Another tradition was begun in the 1860s – federal taxes on breweries to pay for expensive government programs, including war. In July 1, 1862, the Internal Revenue Act placed a tax of one dollar on each barrel of beer sold. The act also required a license from brewers, another source of revenue. The Civil War that had begun the previous year was growing expensive, and Congress needed a secure and quick way to pay for the bloody war. Passage of the Internal Revenue Act had another effect – it led the brewers to unite. On August 21, 1862, they formed what later became the United States Brewers Association.

At first, all of the members of the USBA were from New York. The organization came to be dominated by German brewers from the eastern states, a reflection of the influence of the Germans and their new style of lager beer. The German influence on the USBA was so widespread that proceedings of the association's conventions were published only in German until 1875, when English was added.

Brewing and taxes have been paired since the first tavern breweries were taxed in the Massachusetts colonies in the 1600s. The federal government taxed breweries in the 1860s to pay for the Civil War, but didn't reduce or eliminate the tax when the war ended. Forty years later, with the nation going to war in Cuba, Congress raised the beer tax to $2 a barrel. According to the brewers, the tax raised $15 million in just six months. The amount was almost half of the cost, tabulated at $38 million, for the brief war.

The German brewers, who were now organized within the USBA, lobbied against the tax increase saying it was meant to support the war and not just to increase government revenues. But the tax was not reduced for three years, when it went to $1.60 a barrel in July 1901, and then to $1 the next year.

BREWING GOES INDUSTRIAL

During the 1870–80s, dramatic changes came to brewing on a scale never realized before. These changes took brewing from a cottage enterprise to an industrial process. Virtually every task, from milling and mashing the grain, heating the kettle, and moving the beer to packaging and protecting it underwent dramatic changes.

Steam power made it a more efficient and cleaner source of fuel for the brewing process. Steam changed how the brew kettle was heated, the grain was milled and mashed, and the beer moved around the brewery. Other mechanical inventions came into use in brewing – elevators, pumps, keg washers, and refrigeration to cool the beer

Until refrigeration came into widespread use, ice making and cold storage was a major activity of all lager breweries. Since lager had to be

INTERIOR OF POTH BREWERY, PHILADELPHIA

The Poth Brewery, founded by Fred A. Poth in 1865, became the second largest in Philadelphia's Brewerytown after Bergner & Engel. These illustrations show the size and sophistication of the brewery about 1888 when thousands of workers were employed in the large brewery. Poth was the only brewery in Brewerytown to open after Repeal in 1933. Most of the original building still stands in Philadelphia at 31st and Jefferson Streets. *(Reprinted with permission. Library Company of Philadelphia)*

stored at cold temperatures, ice had to be in the brewery year round. Caves were often dug for storing beer. In the summer, the temperature in the caves may not have been cold enough, so ice was stored in them to chill the beer. During winter, men would cut and chop ice on rivers and lakes and store it in warehouses for use in the brewery in the summer . Tens of thousands of ice blocks were cut and stored by breweries until the 1880s, when refrigeration came into use on an industrial scale.

A demonstration of refrigeration at the Centennial Exhibition in 1876 acquainted breweries with this new development in cooling and storing. The Portner Brewery in Alexandria, Virginia, the Best Brewery in Milwaukee, and Liebmann's Sons Brewery in Brooklyn were pioneers in bring refrigeration into brewing.

The experiments of Louis Pasteur on fermentation led to another major development in bringing consistency and quality to brewing. Heating beer in bottles would kill bacteria or yeast. The process stopped fermentation and prevented spoilage during shipment and storage. By the 1890s, large breweries sent bottled beer traveling down assembly lines where steaming water would bath the bottles and raise the temper-

YUENGLING BREWERY WORKERS ABOUT 1873
Brewing was a labor intensive industry. Workers from Yuengling Brewery worked in the lagering caves inside the coal-rich mountains in Pottsville, Pennsylvania. Barrels of lager would be stored in cold temperatures for months in the mountain caves to produce the clear, clean lager beer preferred by German immigrants. The lager style became the most popular beer in the world by the turn of the century. *(Reprinted with permission. Yuengling Brewery)*

ature to kill yeast or bacteria. Pasteurization protected the beer during transportation or while on shelves and brought a level of consistency never realized before in brewing.

Another improvement in the storage of beer was the replacement of porcelain or metal stoppers with metal crowns fitted with cork seals. By the 1880s, beer was packaged in bottling plants located next to the brewery. The law prevented bottling being done in a brewery. Instead, brewing operations would end with beer being pumped into kegs, sealed with a cork, and shipped across a street to be put into bottles. This expensive, time-consuming requirement was a result of laws that had not changed from the old days of brewing in small operations.

PROHIBITION FORCES GROW

The lager revolution and the industrialization of brewing was accompanied by another force – temperance or prohibition against alcohol. Brewing was becoming a powerful industry dominated by German immigrants. The increase in size and production was accompanied by an anti-German attitude in America. The German brewers in turn grew defensive when their economic motives became intertwined with allegations about their patriotism. In earlier times, temperance groups were dismissed as eccentric trouble makers or religious nuts. But by the 1870s, brewers could no longer ignore temperance's growing political and public support.

After the Civil War, prohibition forces organized their first national convention in 1869. Prohibition appeared as an issue in the Presidential campaign of 1872, when Democrat Horace Greeley ran on a platform of prohibition against Ulysses Grant, who was running for his second term. Despite losing the election, prohibition forces gained new strength when Dr. Dio Lewis, a Boston minister, founded the Women's Crusade. Lewis marched into the barrooms and saloons with hymn singing, prayers, and speeches. Lewis's quirky gesture succeeded in gaining public support, and, in 1874, the Women's Crusade evolved into the Women's Christian Temperance Union (WCTU).

To counter the negative publicity, the brewers argued that brewing made an important contribution to the national economy. They claimed that brewers and distillers paid 55% of the Internal Revenue Tax.[5] Brewery production was nearly 9,000,000 barrels a year, and there were 4,131 breweries in 1873, the highest number ever reached in the history of the country.[6]

NATIONAL BREWERIES EMERGE

The industrialization of brewing not only changed how beer was brewed, but it also ushered in an expanded national market for beer. The era of a small brewery serving all its beer within a few miles of its home changed to one where a brewery could ship beer hundreds and thousands of miles. Beer was no longer delivered in horse-drawn carriages, but in refrigerated railroads cars that crisscrossed the country. This created the nationalization of brewing, a phenomenon that affected all manufacturing industries at the turn of the century.

The industrialization era grew breweries into enormous factories at the expense of smaller operations. The number of breweries declined from more than 4,000 in the 1870s to about 1,500 in 1900.[7] But these breweries were making more beer. Approximately 13 million barrels were produced in 1880, and almost 60 million in 1910. Another landmark was reached by the turn of the century – the million-barrel-a-year brewery. The Pabst Brewery (formerly Best) reached the million barrel level in 1893. In 1900, another Milwaukee brewery, Schlitz, reached that mark and Anheuser-Busch sold just under 1 million barrels the same year.

With all the growth, expansion, and national marketing among breweries, there was a need for additional brewing capacity. An alternative to

ANHEUSER-BUSCH BREWERY, ST. LOUIS, 1880–82

Anheuser-Busch was becoming one of the nation's brewery giants during the 1880s Golden Age of Brewing. In this early photo of the St. Louis brewery complex, the two tallest buildings in the rear are the old brewhouse (1869) and new brewhouse. The tall building with the tower is the malt elevator; the ice storage and refrigeration house are in the rear at the left. (*Reprinted with permission. Anheuser-Busch Brewery*)

buying new equipment and building new breweries was simply to buy other breweries. The era of mergers and consolidations was beginning, a process which lasted late into the 20th century.

One of the largest consolidations took place in Pittsburgh in 1899. Twenty-one breweries agreed to merge into the Pittsburgh Brewing Company. Six of these breweries were relatively large for city breweries – Iron City, Z. Wainwright, Eberhardt & Ober, Winter Brothers, Phoenix, and Straub.[8] Pittsburgh's smaller breweries were liquidated and equipment sold over the course of several years until the only brewery left was the Iron City Brewery on Liberty Avenue.

The Pittsburgh Brewing Company, one of the first to be involved in the 19th-century mergers, continues today as a modern regional brewery making craft beers at the same Liberty Avenue location almost a century after the city-wide consolidation. It is the rare brewery to have survived the cannibalization frenzy that was so much a part of the last 100 years. One foot of Pittsburgh Brewing is in 19th-century brewing history, the other is in the New Age of the craft brewing revival looking to its biggest growth in the 21st century.

Stegmaier Brewing Co., Wilkes-Barre, Pa.

STEGMAIER BREWERY, WILKES-BARRE, PENNSYLVANIA

The valleys and mountains of eastern Pennsylvania were filled with immigrant miners working the coal fields fueling the 19th century Industrial Revolution. Wilkes-Barre's Stegmaier Brewery was the largest brewery in eastern Pennsylvania and its beer was sold throughout eastern Pennsylvania, New York, and New Jersey. Stegmaier fell victim to the popularity of the national breweries after Prohibition and eventually closed its doors in 1974. The building still stands at Market street. A Stegmaier beer is occasionally produced at the Lion Brewery across town. (*Reprinted with permission. The Haydock Collection*)

CARRIE NATION'S CRUSADE

Labor disputes, federal taxes, and industrial growth all affected the evolution of the brewing industry, but no force had a more deleterious impact than temperance. Since the mid-1750s, when the spirits issue aroused efforts to control drinking, concern about the social impact of drinking grew into a national political cause. That cause was represented by many groups with the Anti-Saloon League and the Women's Christian Temperance Union (WCTU) being the most powerful.

A figure to emerge from the temperance movement was Carry Nation, a crusader whose hatchet wielding against speakeasies and saloons in the Midwest made her a media sensation. Nation learned from the success of the Women's Crusade of the 1870s, taking the battle into the streets and saloons. She personified the rabid anti-alcohol forces who wanted to do violent damage to the alcohol industry like Carry Nation inflicted on Kansas saloons.

In 1899, Nation began a one-woman crusade in the small town of Medicine Lodge, Kansas, where she lived with her second husband. She closed the speakeasies in Medicine Lodge and moved on to Kiowa a few miles away where she bludgeoned three saloons and got her picture in newspapers all over the country. Nation moved her crusade to Wichita, Topeka, and all over the country, smashing bottles, barrooms, windows, kegs and anything that smacked of the wicked liquor and beer industry.

Despite fines and imprisonment, Nation carried on her propaganda campaign for more than ten years until she became a caricature of her ideals. Supported by the clergy, she was mocked by the brewers and saloons who baited her with banners proclaiming, "All Nations Welcome But Carry," and Carry Nation cocktails. A troubled soul, Nation fell ill and was ridiculed as a religious nut who claimed she talked to God, Jesus, the Holy Ghost, and the disciples.

Nation's mother, grandmother, uncles, aunts and cousins had been declared insane, and she herself died of "nervous trouble" in 1911. But even in death, Nation found no peace. After Prohibition had become the law of the land in 1920, the largest moonshine still in that part of Missouri was found on her father's old farm near her grave in Belton.[9]

TEMPERANCE BECOMES PROHIBITION

By the turn of the century, nearly every political campaign at the national, state, and local level, had a prohibition plank. Prohibition forces were most effective at the local level first. Working from the

BERGNER & ENGEL, PHILADELPHIA
Philadelphia's Brewerytown was the largest concentration of breweries in the country. Bergner & Engel was the largest brewery in Brewerytown. It was formed from a partnership of Gustav Bergner who began brewing in 1854 and Charles Engel who joined in 1869. Engel had been half of the Engel and Wolf Brewery, the first lager brewery in America. By 1880, the Bergner & Engel Brewery was brewing 250,000 barrels a year. Its Tannhaeuser beer was a well-known national brand sold throughout the East. (*Reprinted with permission. The Haydock Collection*)

local to the state level, prohibition forces were successful in getting nine states to vote "dry" in 1912. In 1914, the number was 16; and in 1916, 23 states were dry, more than half of the United States. This momentum carried to Congress – by 1916, the majority of Congress was sympathetic to the "dry" lobby.

Prohibitionist forces had more than popular sentiment working for them, they also had the shrill jingoistic appeal. Since the majority of brewers were German, it was easy to whip up anti-brewer sentiment with a not-so-subtle attack at the "patriotism" of the German brewers, who, by nature of their heritage, were accused of being sympathetic to the dreaded "Hun" fighting in the trenches in France.

The election of a "dry" Congress in 1916 was followed by a declaration of war on Germany in 1917. One wartime measure dealt with the manufacture and control of food products. The bill proved to be a convenient vehicle to legislate prohibition. When the measure passed on September 8, 1917, it contained an amendment prohibiting the production of distilled spirits. Brewing beer was left to the discretion of President Wilson, who approved the manufacture of beer, but only with an alcohol content of $2^3/4\%$ by weight.

PROHIBITION BECOMES LAW OF THE LAND

The Eighteenth Amendment passed the House on December 18, 1917, by a vote of 181 to 128. It sped through the states and was ratified in 13 months. The Secretary of State announced on January 16, 1919, that the amendment had been ratified by the required number of states and Prohibition would go into effect one year from that date. Showing the strength of neo-prohibition forces around the country, the states continued ratifying the amendment until only two, Rhode Island and Connecticut refused.

In May 1919, as the dreaded day approached, the Volstead Act creating the National Prohibition Act was introduced by Representative Andrew Volstead of Minnesota, Chairman of the House Judiciary Committee. It passed the House and Senate in October but was vetoed by President Wilson because it contained a wartime prohibition section he said was not necessary. Two hours after Wilson's veto message was delivered to Congress, the House overrode his veto. The Senate followed the next day.

Congress set up a Prohibition Unit within the Internal Revenue division of the Treasury Department with an initial appropriation of two million dollars in 1920. The first Prohibition Unit was created with 1,520 agents each receiving an annual salary of $1,680, a wage too low to support a family in any city.[10]

The response to the enforcement of Prohibition was predictable. Legitimate breweries and distilleries found ways to circumvent enforce-

FRANK JONES, PORTSMOUTH, NEW HAMPSHIRE

The Frank Jones Brewery was the largest ale producing brewery in New England. A descendant revived the brewery name and started a craft brewery in Portsmouth in the 1980's. The effort failed, but another local brewery, the Portsmouth Brewpub, bought the equipment at auction in 1993 and resurrected the Jones brewery as the Smuttnynose Brewery. (*Reprinted with permission. The Haydock Collection*)

ment. A few thousand prohibition agents were sadly inadequate to address a nationwide problem and corruption was everywhere. Judges, mayors, city council members, chiefs of police, deputies, and county commissioners were indicted every day during the 13 years when alcohol was banned.

Some breweries closed forever. Large breweries stayed open and made soda, cereal beverages, and near beer. More than 500 breweries continued working, ostensibly to make near beer, a product that had no market before Prohibition. It was easy for breweries to flagrantly abuse Prohibition. Some vessels labeled near beer contained regular beer. Near beer was shipped to speakeasies, followed by clandestine shipments of alcohol that would be injected into the near beer at the speakeasy. The result was beer that could contain from 3% to 15% alcohol. Hangovers were the least physical effect of this "hooch." Seizures and even death came from the unregulated and illegal products of clandestine brewing and distilling.

Another dodge breweries used was to manufacture wort, or unfermented malted barley. Wort was sold openly and transported to basements or alley breweries where the fermentation would begin when a bar of yeast was pitched into the vessel. Again, the quality of the resulting beer was questionable.

Breweries that didn't have a permit to brew near beer were "dismantled" by Prohibition agents. Oftentimes this meant that a prohibition agent would show up, remove a strategic pipe or valve from the brewery, and declare it "dismantled." After the agent left, it would be relatively easy to restore the brewery with a new pipe or rubber hose to get the brewery operational once again.

This flagrant violation of federal law had a profound impact on the country. Legitimate political and legal authorities suffered because of the widespread corruption of public officials from the lowest deputy to the federal bench. Organized crime was well prepared to move into the arena of selling and distributing alcohol and exact a steep profit. With handsome profits so readily available, struggles over territory and product led to violence, bloodshed, blackmail, and terrorism.

It was not America's finest hour. Around the world, the United States was ridiculed as a hypocritical nation which passed self-righteous laws against alcohol and, at the same time, condoned violence and bloodshed to circumvent the law. This hypocritical view was embodied most dramatically in the figure of Al Capone, a violent Chicago thug who exacted heavy duty on the legal system. Only in America could a crime lord of Capone's ilk become a wealthy and influential hero. Chicago had always been a big beer-drinking city, and Capone and his henchmen made millions controlling the city's breweries, which were never idle during Prohibition. The Roaring '20s was that sad chapter in our history when lawlessness became "respectable."

REPEAL BECOMES A REALITY

Opposition to Prohibition had always been widespread but disorganized. By the late 1920s, various groups were coalescing to get rid of the hated law. This required the long, legal route to federal revocation of the 18th amendment. By 1930, the American Legion, labor unions, the Bar Association of New York, the American Bar Association, the Moderation League, the Association Against the Prohibition Amendment, and numerous women's groups called for Repeal. Some of the most prominent business leaders, including all the directors of General Motors, called for ending the disastrous experiment. But the biggest ally of Repeal was the crippling economic depression the country had entered in 1929.

The 1932 presidential election became a debate on Prohibition and Franklin Roosevelt campaigned on a "wet" platform. The support for Repeal had three strong issues in its favor: a crippling economic depression, lack of public support for Prohibition, and the failure and corruption of the unenforceable law.

The House began hearings after Roosevelt was elected on modifying the Volstead Act to allow brewing beer as a non-intoxicating liquor. Since

CARPENTERS & TINNERS AT ANHEUSER-BUSCH, c. 1896

Brewing in the industrial era was more than making beer. Brewing was an industry that employed many trades, such as these carpenters and tinners at Anheuser-Busch's St. Louis brewery prior to the turn of the century. European immigrants were proud of their new country and their German employers. (*Reprinted with permission. Anheuser-Busch Brewery*)

the Volstead Act left the definition of an "intoxicating beverage" to Congress, the body considered and approved 3.2% beer. It passed the House on December 21, 1932, and when Roosevelt was inaugurated, he recommended passage of a modification of the Volstead Act by the Senate. Roosevelt's measure passed Congress, which allowed the sale of 3.2% beer in states that didn't have prohibition, a tax of $5 on the barrel, and a tax of $1,000 per brewery. The Great Experiment was over. Legislation of social behavior had failed.

AN INDUSTRY IN TRANSITION

A slumbering industry began to awaken after the long drought. Those breweries that had switched to making near bear, soft drinks, and derivatives, had made modifications to keep their equipment modernized. There was a rush to begin brewing again, and by June 1933, 31 breweries were operating. A year later, only 756 out of some 1,100 open at the beginning of Prohibition managed to return to brewing.

But after Repeal, changes came to brewing as dramatic as those of the 19th-century Industrial age. The post-Prohibiton era proved to be highly competitive and ruthless. Household names of yesterday became extinct in the present.

Advancements in technology made it more efficient to put beer in bottles and cans for the home trade. Refrigerators in homes made domestic beer consumption more available than before Prohibition. Draught sales, popular before Prohibition, declined from a high of 75% of production in 1934 to 48% in 1941 when package sales reached 52%.[11]

The first sale of beer in cans was in Richmond in 1935 with the American Can Company working with the Krueger Brewery in New Jersey. Within a few years, the major manufacturers of metal cans had worked out deals with the major brewers to put their beer in cans. A similar change took place with one-way glass bottles, which were lighter, cheaper, and more efficient than the larger bottles been had been packaged in before Prohibition.

Beer consumption finally reached pre-Prohibiton levels in 1940. This was accomplished with half the number of breweries, about 700. Six breweries were now selling more than 1 million barrels a year: Anheuser-Busch, Schlitz, Pabst, Ballantine, Schaefer, and Ruppert.[12]

Even though production was up, per capita consumption had declined. Brewers blamed this on the increase of the barrel tax from $5 to $6 in July, 1940. With war in Europe, this Defense Tax was seen as a national defense issue, despite its impact on the smaller brewers who found it difficult to absorb. The war-time years saw a boost in production from 53 million barrels in 1940 to almost 80 million at the end of the war in 1945.

The postwar years saw breweries expand westward to serve the population shift to the sun belt. Consolidation within the industry saw the numbers of breweries decline until 1981 when only 41 breweries were operating. With all of the dramatic changes going on in manufacturing, transportation, taxes, and packaging, it was the only the strongest—and biggest—who could survive.

CLOSING THE CIRCLE

The era of the efficient, giant brewing factory reached its peak in the mid-20th century. Brewing was more scientific, efficient, cheap, and predictable than it ever had been. The beer it turned out was the most scientifically consistent, but geared to the perceived tastes interpreted by marketing forces. What it wasn't, was interesting, tasteful, or varied.

A nation that had been founded with small brewers making numerous beer styles had become a giant industry brewing the same style of pilsener beer in every brewery. Efficiency and profits had been gained at the price of creativity and taste.

But consumers are not always predictable and uniform. A nation that had once had a variety of beer styles was in search of change by the 1960s. Consumers discovered the merits of numerous beer styles with import beers and showed their support by paying premium prices for the products. But why couldn't American breweries make these specialty beers?

The circle was closing. A nation founded on small, colonial craft breweries was returning to its origins. A craft brewing revolution was being born in the shadow of brewing factories. The pendulum was swinging. A brewing heritage was about to be rediscovered. Craft beers were coming back.

CHAPTER TWO FOOTNOTES

1. Baron, Stanley. *Brewed in America: A History of Beer and Ale in the United States,* Little Brown, & Co., Boston, 1962, p. 176.

2. *Ibid.,* p. 177.

3. *Ibid.,* p. 189.

4. *Ibid.,* p. 211.

5. *Ibid.,* p. 225.

6. *Ibid.,* p. 226.

7. *Ibid.,* p. 257.

8. *Ibid.,* p. 271.

9. Asbury, Herbert. *The Great Illusion: An Informal History of Prohibition,* Doubleday, Garden City, New York, 1950, p. 120.

10. *Ibid.,* p. 135.

11. Baron, p. 326.

12. *Ibid.,* p. 331.

~ CHAPTER THREE ~

A BEER CULTURE EMERGES IN THE BIG EAST

In an earlier period of our history, beer was a vital part of the fabric of the nation, principally as a source of food and a means for social lubrication. In the Industrial era of the 19th and early 20th centuries, beer was a part of the national economy – with brewing factories, beer shipped nationwide and promoted in advertising and the national media. Beer was a billion-dollar product sold around the nation in restaurants, pubs, taverns, markets, liquor, and convenience stores. It was big business.

But beer at the end of the 20th century has taken on a new dimension. We have a culture of beer developing. Today's beer culture exists apart from the national brewing industry and its advertising. Those involved in the new beer culture have little connection to the major breweries and their products. The culture thrives within the craft brewing industry that produces only 1% of the beer brewed in the country. The beer culture allows one to be participant, hobbyist, entrepreneur, collector – and even brewer.

First of all, what is a beer culture? Briefly, it is loosely organized groups of individuals who participate in activities with which they have affinity. It's more than a hobby, it's a way of life. Beer invites people to socialize together. People tend to drink beer in groups, and when those groups get together, they're likely to talk about beer rather than just sports, politics, the weather, or work. A beer culture, then, is a range of activities where members share their common interest – beer.

BIRTH OF A BIG EAST BEER CULTURE

The Big East beer culture was in its infancy by the mid-1980s. Home-brewing has always been a bellwether that a groundswell is building for specialty beers. Big East homebrewers were active in the 1980s and many had made the trip out to the West Coast to visit the early craft breweries. When they returned, their brewing activities took on a new level of enthusiasm.

A culture of any kind requires that the members of the culture have a way to be informed. The Big East beer culture depends upon the four brewspapers that report bimonthly on beer events in their area. By the 1990s, the first Big East brewspapers appeared – *Yankee Brew News* first appeared in Boston in 1989, *BarleyCorn* in the Washington-Baltimore area in 1990, and *Ale Street News* in New York in 1992. Brewspapers are part of that great American tradition of the free press spreading the word and being a part of a new order. Without exaggeration, the modern brewspapers are the descendants of the Federalist Papers and stepchildren of the First Amendment.

Beer dinners hosted by restaurants and hotels are another manifesta-tion of a beer culture. Beer dinners were already happening in the late 1980s and have spread to some of the Big East's most prestigious organi-zations – the Culinary Institute of America, Waldorf Astoria Hotel in New York, Clyde's Restaurants and the Smithsonian Institute in Washington, and Walt Disney World in Orlando. These organizations certainly would not promote beer-related activities unless their audience would financially support them. By all accounts, the beer events have been very successful.

The active homebrewers, the early craft breweries, beer dinners, and brewspapers naturally led to that last example of the Big East beer cul-ture phenomenon – beer festivals. The first beer festivals were held in Boston and Pennsylvania in 1992. Since then, beer festivals have spread throughout New England and the mid-Atlantic States.

The Big East Beer culture is thriving and growing. If you haven't already taken part, the opportunity will come to you soon. Just read on – you're almost there.

HOMEBREWERS

Scratch a homebrewer and you'll find a craft brewing "wannabe." They may not have the money or time to become a full-fledged craft brewer, but they belong to the same genus and species. They brew regularly, read voraciously about their field, and get together with like-minded brews brothers to shmooze about their favorite topic. And they're evange-lists! They want everybody to drink good beer.

Some of the first craft brewers – Jim Kollar at Chesbay, Matthew Reich at New Amsterdam, William Newman at Newman's, and Greg Noonan at

Vermont Pub and Brewery–began as homebrewers before making the leap into commercial brewing. Most craft brewers working today had their epiphany while sweating over that first batch of homebrew.

Homebrewers come in all sizes, shapes, colors, and political orientations. But that doesn't mean a thing, because their love of beer is what unites them. Homebrewing has grown from a garage-and-basement enterprise to a major segment in the industry with homebrew clubs, newsletters, magazines, beer tastings, retail stores, and brew-your-own shops popping up to supply them. They are a cottage industry and growing every year.

Homebrewers are the advance guard of the craft brewing movement. They're more than customers for craft breweries–they also provided a network of consumers and dispense brewing "intelligence" to other consumers, the media, and retailers.

The newest wrinkle in homebrewing is the U-Brew shops that rent time on brewing vessels in a retail storefront. Customers come in and brew with modern equipment that they may not be able to afford or have room to install at home. Homebrewers brew a batch, return in a few days to shift the working beer into storage vessels, and then return to taste their brewing gems. The U-brew shops began in Canada where beer is heavily taxed. The advantage for homebrewers is that it lets them brew with equipment similar to that operating at the local brewpub or micro-brewery. Two of these shops will open in Boston in 1994.

Homebrewers love little more than showing off their wares (and offering samples) to fellow homebrewers. They love to get together to drink and talk about their favorite beers–usually theirs. One of the many delights of homebrewers is their sense of humor. An indication of this is the names they give their homebrew clubs. Some of the choicer names of Big East homebrew clubs are the Wort Processors (Boston), Connecticut Beer Nuts, MALT (Maine Ale and Lager Tasters), Chicken City Ale Raisers (Georgia), TRASH (Three River Alliance of Serious Homebrewers), and BURP (Brewers United for Real Potables), Washington.

Buy a kit, pick up some supplies, scrub down your kitchen, and brew up a batch. Then join a club where they're having all the fun. Who knows where this new hobby will lead you? It's a rare craft brewery that doesn't have homebrewers dropping by regularly to live out their fantasy of working in a brewery. Life can't get much better than that.

Viva la zymurgistas!

BREWSPAPERS

No one need suffer for timely information about the Big East beer culture. With four brewspaper and a newsletter and magazine covering the industry from New England to Florida, the newsstands and mailboxes are bulging with beer publications every month. And the information is excellent – entertaining, timely, interesting, and informative. Today's beer readers tend to be well-educated, work in a professional occupation, travel for business and pleasure, and are eager to be involved in beer events. They are busy and want to know how they can participate.

Yankee Brew News

Yankee Brew News was started by Don Gosselin in 1989 as a modest newsletter for the homebrew shop where he worked. Gosselin's one-color, 8-page newsletter has evolved into a three-color, 24-page sheet covering the frenzied New England brewing scene. *YBN* is challenged to cover the area with the greatest concentration of craft breweries in the country.

Yankee Brew News started chronicling the New England scene when it consisted of five pioneering brewpubs in 1989: Cambridge, Vermont, Commonwealth, Northampton, and Geary's. The task is more demanding today with 45 diverse breweries, a sophisticated readership, and a beer culture rivaled only by the Northwest, where craft brewing began in the early 1980s.

The New England area is small and close knit. *Yankee Brew News* has the privilege of reporting on more breweries, beer festivals, homebrew gatherings, and beer events in a smaller geographic regional than any other beeriodical. *Yankee Brew News's* strength are the feature stories and reviews of New England breweries and the region's enthusiasm for local beers.

Since starting the homebrew newsletter, Gosselin has delegated staff responsibilities to Brett Peruzzi, Dann Paquette, Ken Spolsino and a crew of stringers. They're going to have their hands full for a few years as breweries keep popping up throughout New England. Bimonthly circulation is 50,000. (Yankee Brew News, P.O. Box 520250, Winthrop, MA 02152-0005. 617-846-5521. $12.95 for year subscription.)

Ale Street News

Ale Street News, started by Tony Forder and Jack Babin, premiered in 1992 and covers the congested urban corridor from New England to Washington. This is the largest urban concentration in the country: Boston, New York, Philadelphia, Baltimore, and Washington, D.C., and the suburban sprawl from the Atlantic coast to inland farmlands and mountains. Total population of the region is some 40 million readers–and a lot of beer drinkers.

Although the Ale Street News region is heavily populated, the craft brewing movement is less diverse than the other areas in the Big East. The New England area has a mixture of urban and campus brewpubs, quaint family cottage breweries, and rural brewpubs. The territory covered by Ale Street News consists of several contract breweries, regional breweries, and a few urban brewpubs. Densely populated urban areas have been slow to develop a diverse brewing community. New York City has three brewpubs and two contract breweries. Maine has eleven breweries.

The 40-page Ale Street News is the second largest in pages and first in circulation in the Big East. It covers the Mid-Atlantic brewery openings, beer festivals, beer dinners, and personality profiles sprinkled with features on Belgian beers, Canadian craft brewing, and tastings of organic and ice beers. Michael Jackson and Alan Eames are contributors. Bimonthly circulation is 70,000 per issue. (Ale Street News, P.O. Box 1125, Maywood, NJ 07607. 201-368-9100. $14.95 for year subscription.)

BarleyCorn

BarleyCorn was started by George Rivers and Steve Cavagnaro (who is no longer with the venture) in 1990 in the Washington suburb of Vienna, VA. The Washington area is one of the more beer sophisticated centers in the Big East, despite the fact that it has only a modest number of craft breweries. BarleyCorn's coverage stretches up to New York and includes the Mid-Atlantic states focusing on Philadelphia, Baltimore, and Washington. This territory is much the same as that covered by Ale Street News, which has reportedly caused a little tension between the two publications. But there's plenty of news for both to cover without stepping on toes.

BarleyCorn has some of the most creative graphics of the brewspapers and a stable of excellent beer writers who were researching beer before the craft brewing explosion. Martin Wooster contributes book reviews, and Greg Kitsock handles the feature articles such as baseball and beer

CELEBRATING & EXPLORING THE BREWING ARTS

and the Presidents and beer. *BarleyCorn* also publishes feature articles that go beyond the standard craft brewery opening and beer festivals. Recent articles on regional breweries, indigenous beers of the world, women and beer, labeling, and blending beers are some of the best things being written about beer anyplace. A first class publication. Bi-monthly circulation is 40,000. (*BarleyCorn*, P.O. Box 2328 Vienna, VA 22042. 703-573-8970. $15.00 for year subscription.)

Southern Draft Brew News

The newest entry into brewspaper journalism is *Southern Draft Brew News*, whose premier edition appeared at the end of 1993. Published in Florida, *Southern Draft Brew News* has targeted that vast Southeast beer wasteland from North Carolina to Florida and west to Arkansas and Louisiana. *Southern Draft* covers a lot of territory, but the number and variety of breweries is not great – yet. Florida has a respectable number of brewpubs, North Carolina has seven, but then it's far afield to Kentucky, Tennessee, Louisiana, and Alabama, which together total about a dozen

breweries. Georgia and South Carolina have yet to pass laws allowing brewpubs. We're not talking drastic social legislation or anti-religious practices – just good beer locally brewed. A shame, really.

Clearly, *Southern Draft* is taking the long view. Beer has always been popular in the south, but its the generic lawnmower beers that strike despair in the hearts of craft beer lovers. The lighter pilsener beers popular in the South most likely have a lot to do with the hot, sticky weather the region suffers through most of the year.

But *Southern Draft* has patience; the Southern Sleeping Beer Giant will eventually awaken. The South never had a brewing tradition like the East or Midwest, but it does have Atlanta, Charlotte, New Orleans, Miami, and Nashville where consumers are discovering the craft brewing culture. Jerry Gengler started the 32-page *Southern Draft* with help from Sara and Phil Doersam who contribute articles on cooking and home brewing. Bimonthly circulation is 40,000. (*Southern Draft Brew News*, 702 Salfish Road, Winter Springs, FL 32708. 407-327-9451. $15 for year subscription.)

All About Beer

Not to be slighted are two Big East publications published in the Southeast near wasteland of craft brewing. *All About Beer*, published by Dan Bradford, is located in Raleigh, North Carolina. Bradford was Marketing Director for the Great American Beer Festival in Boulder for its first 10 years. After Dan married and moved to North Carolina, he bought the California-based magazine from Bosak Publishing and moved it across the country. Mike Bosak and his wife, Bunny, had guided *All About Beer* in its first 15-year history when the craft brewing movement was beginning. When the Bosaks started publishing, the biggest thing in beer was the thrilling "Tastes Great...Less Filling" debate. We've come a long way.

In its new location in the North Carolina Research Triangle area, *All About Beer* has gone through a major redesign, added new writers, and put a bright, exciting face on the magazine. There has been a shift from carrying international brewing stories to more on North American craft brewing, a field that's getting more crowded by the day. (*All About Beer*, Chataqua Publications, 1627 Marion Avenue, Durham, NC 27705. 800-977-BEER. $25.50 for year subscription.)

On Tap

On *Tap* Newsletter set the standard for beer newsletters. Published since 1989 by Steve Johnson in Clemson, South Carolina, the bimonthly *On Tap* is frequently the first to report on craft brewing happenings around the country. Steve has a network of contributors who keep him posted on the latest openings and closings. They supply him with articles whenever they visit breweries around the world.

For its first six years, Johnson's newsletter was called *World Beer Review*. He changed the name and shifted his focus from a mixture of international and domestic brewing news to the American craft brewing movement. *On Tap*'s beer ratings are often quoted in beer publications or by breweries, a testimony to *On Tap*'s credibility. Steve also publishes *On Tap* regional books for craft breweries around the country, dividing them into two editions, east and west of the Mississippi. (*On Tap Newsletter*, P.O. Box 71, Clemson, SC 29633. 803-654-3360. $18.50 for year subscription.)

BEER FESTIVALS

Beer festivals have become a major outgrowth of the craft brewing movement. A beer festival is an enthusiastic crowd usually gathered in a beautiful setting (when weather permits), enjoying superb beers with friends, good food, and a little music. Beer festivals are a true celebration of the craft brewing experience. What a way to spend an afternoon. Try it sometime – you'll join the beer culture on the spot.

The first two Big East beer festivals were the Boston Brewers Festival in May 1992 and the Great Eastern Microbrewery Invitational at the Stoudt Brewery in Adamstown the next month. The sold-out events were a signal to organizers that it was time to catch up with the West where beer festivals had been popular for years. The Oregon Brewers Festival in 1993 attracted some 60,000 over a July weekend.

By 1993, numerous beer events and festivals were scheduled in Vermont, Boston, New York, Washington, Baltimore, and Florida. Beer festivals soon will be spreading to other towns – Syracuse, Portland, Richmond, Raleigh, and Tampa. The future will likely see beer festivals in almost any town that has a connection to craft brewing.

The spring, summer, and fall are when major beer festivals are popular. A few festivals likely to be scheduled annually are:

APRIL	Southeastern Microbrew Invitational, Raleigh, NC
MAY	Boston Brewers Festival, World Trade Center, Boston 617-547-6311
JUNE	Great Eastern Invitational Microbrewery Festival, Stoudt Brewery, Adamstown, PA 215-484-4385
	Ironworks Festival of Beers, Pittsburgh 412-276-0122
JULY	WMFE beer festival, Orlando 407-273-2300

	Great New England Brewers Festival, Northampton, Massachusetts 413-584-2079
SEPTEMBER	New York Beer Fest, Brooklyn
	Vermont Brewers Festival, Burlington
	Sugarbush Brewers Festival, Warren, Vermont
	Walt Disney World Beer Festival, Orlando
OCTOBER	Myrtle Beach, South Carolina 919-579-8985
	Rhode Island International Beer Expo 401-0274-3234

Communities all throughout the Big East are likely to schedule beer festivals, beer dinners, and tastings throughout the year. For complete information, consult your local brewspaper or inquire at a craft brewery.

THE CRYSTAL BALL

Beer has been a part of American history for centuries, and the emerging beer culture is testimony that we're rediscovering our brewing heritage. With new breweries opening each month, the popularity of beer festivals, new beers being brewed, beer dinners and homebrewing events, the Big East beer culture is going to grow dramatically over the next few years. Millions will be waking up to the new and exciting world of craft brewing and discover our long history with beer.

If you haven't noticed already, you'll hear people enthusiastically talking about beers and breweries the way they usually discuss new restaurants, politics, or sports. Breweries are becoming that big–just visit a local brewery, homebrew shop, beer retailer, or go to a beer festival. You'll catch the fever. And if you haven't already, you'll join the beer culture. You won't regret it.

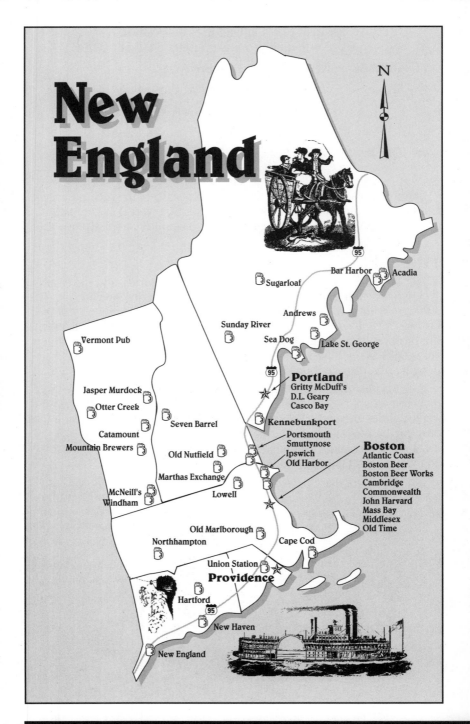

New England

N

Sugarloaf

Bar Harbor   Acadia

Andrews

Sunday River

Sea Dog   Lake St. George

Vermont Pub

Portland
Gritty McDuff's
D.L. Geary
Casco Bay

Jasper Murdock

Otter Creek

Seven Barrel

Kennebunkport

Catamount

Mountain Brewers

Portsmouth
Smuttynose
Ipswich
Old Harbor

Old Nutfield

Boston
Atlantic Coast
Boston Beer
Boston Beer Works
Cambridge
Commonwealth
John Harvard
Mass Bay
Middlesex
Old Time

Marthas Exchange

McNeill's
Windham

Lowell

Old Marlborough

Northhampton

Cape Cod

Union Station
Providence

Hartford

New Haven

New England

HARTFORD BREWERY
35 Pearl Street
Hartford, CT 06103   203-246-BEER

President: Phil Hopkins
Brewer: Les Sinnock
Equipment: 7-barrel Peter Austin system
Opened: August 16, 1991

Phil Hopkins and Les Sinnock each had 10 years homebrewing experience when they decided to pool their experience and open a brewpub. They apprenticed at Geary's Brewpub in Portland, Maine, under Alan Pugsley, who had set up many American and English brewing systems.

With this background, Hopkins and Sinnock chose to brew English-style ales and purchased a brewing system that once toiled at the Frog and Frigate Brewery in England. It took them four years to change state legislation and local zoning regulations to be able to set up the first brewpub in Connecticut.

Hartford Brewery is in the Gold Building near the old State House and Civic Center. It is the only brewpub in the state. All of Hartford's ales are unfiltered and unpasteurized.

Arch Amber: *a stock ale*
Pitbull Golden: *a stock ale*

1992:   200 barrels
1993:   500 barrels

 ## NEW ENGLAND BREWING
25 Commerce Street
Norwalk, CT 06850   203-866-1339

President: Marcia King
Brewers: Phil Markowski and Ron Page
Equipment: Fabricated at family chemical company
Opened: February 1990

Marcia King and her husband, Richard, were on vacation in 1988 in Vermont when they tried a beer from the Catamount Brewery in White River Junction. The Kings were so intrigued by the idea of a craft brewery in New England that they thought it was something for them to consider. Richard had been managing a family specialty chemical plant for many years, and the Kings were looking for a new business venture.

Marcia spent a year researching the craft brewing industry and came up with the idea to start a brewpub in Danbury. That project never came to fruition because Connecticut's economy took a disastrous plunge in the late 1980s and the Kings decided to hold off. They still thought the idea

would work, but switched from starting up a brewpub to building a microbrewery in their hometown of Norwalk. The King family was well known and the city fathers were thrilled at the prospect of a small manufacturing plant opening during a time of high unemployment.

The Kings used the name New England Brewing because of strong regional pride and the fact that there had been many local breweries in the region during much of the 19th and 20th centuries. When construction was going on at their site, builders found bottles from the New England Brewery that had operated in Hartford for nearly 100 years.

The Kings eventually chose a site that was a former grain storehouse on the Norwalk River. The brewing equipment was designed and constructed by workers at King's chemical plant a few blocks away. A used bottling line was purchased from the Upper Canada Brewery in Ontario. The brewery is squeezed into the ground floor and spills out onto the back and into a parking lot. This limited space makes it difficult and uncomfortable to brew during the cold, snowy winters New England is well known for. The brewery offices upstairs are just as cramped.

But the New England brewing team won't have to suffer much longer–hope is in sight. A dream brewery is under construction a few miles away in historic downtown South Norwalk. The city is attempting to attract tourists with a new Maritime Center and related shops and restaurants recalling the atmosphere of a 19th-century New England whaling center. The new 20,000 sq. ft. New England Brewery may open as early as 1994 with a brewpub, museum, gift shop, brewery, and bottling line. Production capacity will be 15,000 barrels / year.

Brewers Ron Page and Phil Markowski have decades of homebrewing experience. Page built a complete basement brewhouse with lagering refrigerators and a restaurant range for heating his brew kettle. He won New England Homebrewer of the Year in 1985 and has earned seven first place awards at nationally sanctioned homebrewing competitions. Markowski began homebrewing in 1984 while he worked as an electronics engineer. He won numerous awards in the late 1980s and specialized in Belgian Saison and steam beer (which became the recipe for Atlantic

Amber). Markowski found the steam beer recipe in an article in Western Brewer dated February 15, 1898. He has taken courses at the Siebel Institute and the University of California at Davis since joining New England in 1989.

Atlantic Amber: *derived from a steam beer recipe researched by Markowski; bottom-fermented at warm temperature using two-row English barley and Northern Brewer, Mt. Hood, and Cascade hops. Medium-bodied with well balanced taste and an aftertaste of a copper ale. Gold medal winner in Dusseldorf altbier category at 1993 Great American Beer Festival*
Stock Ale: *a rich, golden ale from the traditional regional style popular in the 19th century; brewed with American two-row malts and Perle, Tettenang, Northern Brewer, Hallertau and Cascade hops*
Oatmeal Stout: *brewed with eight malts, wheat and barley flakes, Northern Brewer and Tettenang hops; medium-bodied with thick head and slight chocolate aftertaste*
Holiday Ale: *brewed with English malts, roasted barley and small amounts of cinnamon, nutmeg, and vanilla beans*

1991: 2,000 barrels
1992: 2,450 barrels
1993: 3,200 barrels

 NEW HAVEN BREWING
458 Grand Avenue
New Haven, CT 06513   203-772-2739

President: Blair Potts
Brewer: Blair Potts
Equipment: 15-barrel JV Northwest system
Opened: September 1989

New Haven Brewery is as much a philosophical expression as an entrepreneurial venture. Although they have a casual, laid back attitude more typical of a California software firm, the brewers at New Haven are deadly serious about the business of selling beer and making a profit. But they want to have fun along the way and not give up their eccentricity. After all, if they weren't brewing beer, they'd have to get a real job.

New Haven Brewery is in an old 21,000 sq. ft. warehouse that used to be a steamship terminal two miles from downtown. The neighborhood doesn't look like they'll have to worry about condos moving in anytime soon. The offices have an unkempt, college fraternity appearance, with music blaring from a plastic radio in the corner, old newspapers lying around, empty beer bottles on the floor, and cartoons and Polaroid photos tacked on the walls. Any mother who has suffered through the teenage years will be right at home.

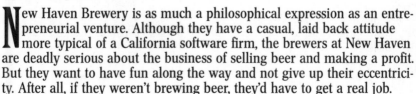

But this irreverent and sloppy appearance ends at the door to the brewery. Stainless steel brewing vessels shine, the floors are spotless, and sanitation rules. After all, beer is brewed in stainless steel vessels and not on desktops cluttered with coffee cups, ashtrays, fast food containers, and last week's newspapers.

This karma of New Haven may come from the eclectic background of the workers. Office manager Jim Gordon was in the wine distribution business before he got into brewing. He is philosophical about craft brewing and where it fits in the social and cultural fabric of the country. Brewer Blair Potts studied history at Yale and found a kinship with Thomas Jefferson, who wrote about individual enterprise as the foundation of a democratic society. "Brewing is an art, the science is only helpful," Potts says when asked about his approach to brewing. Potts has tested all of New Haven's beers on his homebrew equipment and has no formal brewing background except studying brewing texts and consulting with other brewers.

Economic recovery is coming slow to Connecticut, and craft brewing has not yet found its niche. New Haven Brewing will go out of state in 1994 and sell in the Big East states south to Virginia. Defense cutbacks hit the state hard, and unemployment ranks as one of the highest in the country. On top of that, the corporate offices for Heineken, Labatts, Bass, and Guinness are in Connecticut, and they work out deals with wholesalers to have their beers prominently featured in the local restaurants, taverns, and hotels.

Elm City Connecticut Ale: *60% of sales come from this house beer; a brown ale, more like an English mild ale, mildly malty with a short finish*
Elm City Golden Ale: *a slightly sweet, fruity ale with a clean, hop finish*
Blackwell Stout: *named after the black Labrador dog adopted by the brewery; a sweet, caramel tasting stout, deep ruby color, with slight coffee aftertaste*
Belle Dock: *a barley wine; ruby colored with a rich, malty sweetness, well balanced with a dry finish*
Mr. Mike's Light Ale: *a wheat beer brewed with 33% wheat malt; 92 calories per bottle*

1991: 3,805 barrels
1992: 4,200 barrels
1993: 4,305 barrels

ACADIA BREWING/LOMPOC BREWPUB
30 Rodick Street
Bar Harbor, ME 04609   207-288-9392

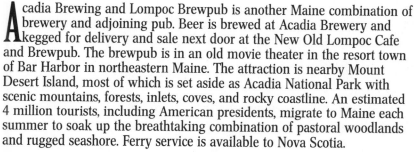

Co-owners: Jon Hubbard and Doug Maffucci
Brewer: Roger Normand
Equipment: 2-barrel system from diverse sources
Opened: May 1991

Acadia Brewing and Lompoc Brewpub is another Maine combination of brewery and adjoining pub. Beer is brewed at Acadia Brewery and kegged for delivery and sale next door at the New Old Lompoc Cafe and Brewpub. The brewpub is in an old movie theater in the resort town of Bar Harbor in northeastern Maine. The attraction is nearby Mount Desert Island, most of which is set aside as Acadia National Park with scenic mountains, forests, inlets, coves, and rocky coastline. An estimated 4 million tourists, including American presidents, migrate to Maine each summer to soak up the breathtaking combination of pastoral woodlands and rugged seashore. Ferry service is available to Nova Scotia.

The Lompoc Brewpub's atmosphere is eclectic, somewhere between an intimate cafe and waterfront pub, with a few bohemian touches. The menu is similar to modest pubs found in seaports where Mediterranean cuisines have found a home. The spicy, international dishes reportedly match up well with the ales served on premise.

Brewpub menu: *diverse offerings of Middle East, Italian, and Greek dishes*

Bar Harbor Real Ale: *a sweet brown ale*
Acadia Pale Ale: *British-style bitter*
Coal Porter
Tree Frog Stout: *dry stout*
Ginger Wheat
Blueberry Ale

1991:   100 barrels
1992:   200 barrels
1993:   N/A

ANDREW'S BREWING

RFD 1. Box 4975
Lincolnville, ME 04849   207-763-3305

President/Brewer: Andrew Hazen
Equipment: 5-barrel locally fabricated system
Opened: November 1992

A ndy Hazen had been a homebrewer for 10 years when he made the decision to go commercial. He had been a woodworker in his earlier career and built an addition to his farmhouse outside Lincolnville, population 1,500, for his "cottage" brewery. Hazen's original system was a tiny 1/2 barrel brewery.

Andrew's beer is available only in kegs, but a bottling line is planned in the future.

Old St. Nick Porter is named after Hazen's dog.

Old St. Nick Porter
Andrew's Brown
Andrew's Old English Ale
Andrew's India Pale Ale

1993:   100 barrels

BAR HARBOR BREWING

Route 3, P.O. Box 63
Bar Harbor, ME 04609   207-288-4592

Brewed and bottled by the
Bar Harbor Brewing Company
BAR HARBOR, MAINE

Co-owners:
Tod & Suzi Foste.
Brewer: Tod Foster
Equipment: 2-barrel Pierre
Rajotte system
Opened: July 1990

T he husband and wife team of Tod and Suzi Foster, home-brewer and restaurauteur, began their family brewery in the basement of their farmhouse outside Bar Harbor. The Fosters also run the Acadia Meadow B & B at their farm during the summer. In the winter of 1994, they moved the brewery south of downtown Bar Harbor.

The Fosters plan to stick with their modest 2-barrel Canadian system and develop sales along Maine's northern coast before expanding out of state, which would be impossible with their small system. They currently have 50 accounts in Downeast Maine from Portland to Bar Harbor.

Bar Harbor's two beers are sold in 22-oz. bottles with the colorful labels drawn by a local artist showing scenes around picturesque Bar Harbor. Thunder Hole Ale is named for a cove in the Acadia National Park where the waves slam against a rocky outcrop producing a spout of foaming surf. Bar Harbor Brewing also makes root beer from a concentrate.

Cadillac Mountain Stout: *a sweet Imperial stout*
Thunder Hole Ale: *a brown ale*
Harbor Light Ale: *a pale ale*

1991:   61 barrels
1992:   130 barrels
1993:   110 barrels

 CASCO BAY BREWING
57 Industrial Road
Portland, ME 04103   207-729-2020

Co-owners: Mike LaCharite & Bob Wade
Brewer: Mike LaCharite
Equipment: 20-barrel DME system
Opened: April 1994

Casco Bay Brewing opened in April 1994 selling kegs and 12- and 22-oz. bottles only in Maine. Founder Mike LaCharite is a veteran home-brewer and former president of MALT, Maine Ale, and Lager Tasters, homebrew club. He earned his credentials from the Siebel Brewing Institute in Chicago.

LaCharite tested his beers on a home-built, 15-gallon brewery in his basement in Brunswick. Cofounder Bob Wade is also a homebrewer who worked for the Hannaford Brothers supermarket chain. Casco Bay's beers are named after the Indian word for Maine's tallest mountain.

An oatmeal stout and raspberry ale will be Casco Bay's first seasonal beers after the brewery is fully operational.

Capacity at Casco Bay will be 3,000–4,000 barrels/year when fully operational by the end of the 1994. The brewery will be only the second in Maine capable of selling draft and bottles throughout New England. Many of Maine's cottage breweries and brewpubs produce only token amounts for sale outside the immediate community where they are brewed.

Casco Bay also plans to have a gift shop selling brewery related items to the thousands of tourists who visit Maine every summer.

Katahdin Golden: *a cream ale*
Katahdin Red Ale: *an Irish red ale*

D. L. GEARY BREWING
38 Evergreen Drive
Portland, ME 04103   207-878-2337

Co-owners: David & Karen Geary
Brewer: David Geary
Equipment: 24-barrel Peter Austin designed system
Opened: December 10, 1986

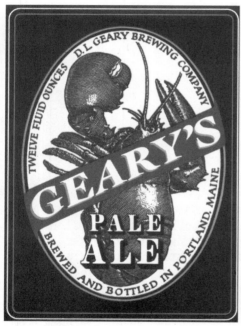

David Geary is one of the Big East's brewing pioneers. He studied brewing in England and Scotland working in a half-dozen breweries including Traquair House in Scotland and the Ringwood Brewery in Hampshire. His brewery was manufactured in Dorset and designed by Peter Austin, the well-known British pub brewer.

Geary was New England's first craft brewery when it opened in 1986. Dave has trained many brewers who have gone on to open or brew at breweries in New England. Although they may be considered competitors, Geary considers it his professional responsibility to repay the courtesy English and Scottish brewers gave him when he was eager to learn brewing. In turn, the brewers who work with Geary are consistently loyal and proud of their connection with Maine's legendary brewer.

Geary will be going through an expansion in 1994–95 funded by a $200,000 investment financed by a local bank. The addition of a 50-barrel brew kettle in a 5,000 sq. ft. addition to the original brewery will increase capacity to 25,000 barrels/year (up from 10,000 barrels) when fully operational.

Geary's beers are available in bottles and kegs in fifteen Big East states, with 85% sold in Maine and New England. Most Maine taverns and restaurants carry Geary's ales.

Geary's Pale Ale: *a English-style pale ale in the tradition of Burton-on-Trent beers, copper-colored, well-hopped, with a smooth, fruity aftertaste*
Hampshire Special Ale: *an English-style strong ale, full-bodied, with an accented hoppy palate; available "only when the weather sucks" from November through April; brewed with two-row English malts, Cascade, Mt. Hood, and East Kent Goldings hops*

1991: 5,300 barrels
1992: 6,200 barrels
1993: 7,200 barrels

 GRITTY MCDUFF'S
396 Fore Street
Portland, ME 04101   207-772-2739

Co-owners: Ed Stebbins & Richard Pfeffer
Brewer: Ed Stebbins
Equipment: 7-barrel Peter Austin system
Opened: July 1988

Gritty McDuff's opened in Portland in 1988 as Maine's first brewpub and one of the best beer pubs in the state. It is located in the restored granite building in the Old Port district. The interior of exposed brick lends a comfortable, at-home neighborhood pub atmosphere.

Brewer Ed Stebbins learned homebrewing as a teenager in England when his Dad gave him a homebrewing kit as a gift. Gritty McDuff's sells 5-liter "growlers" for take home trade in their gift shop.

Brewpub menu: *pubfare*

Black Fly Stout
Sebago Light Ale
McDuff's Vest Bitter
Lion's Pride: *brown ale*
Summer Wheat

1991: 1,000 barrels
1992: 1,204 barrels
1993: 1,569 barrels

**KENNEBUNKPORT BREWING/
FEDERAL JACK'S BREWPUB**
8 Western Avenue, #6
Kennebunk, ME 04043   207-967-4311

President: Fred Forsley
Brewer Paul Hendry
Equipment: 7-barrel Peter Austin system
Opened: June 1992

The Kennebunkport brewery is in the harbor at Kennebunk where former President Bush still summers with Secret Service escorts, dogs, and grandchildren in tow. The brewery shares space with Federal Jack's Brewpub, a popular neighborhood saloon patronized by tourists in the summer and locals who wait for the camera and souvenir-laden crowds to thin out in September. Owner Fred Forsley is a Portland real estate developer who saw the commercial potential of having a brewery in the renovated Shipyard mall, which was an 18th-century shipyard.

The brewpub has a familiar nautical atmosphere, with polished brass, natural woods, and paintings of old ships. Brewing consultant Alan Pugsley, who has set up numerous Big East brewing systems, was the guiding force at Kennebunkport. Peter Austin Brewing systems, Pugsley's equipment company, installed the 7-barrel system. Brewer Paul Hendry worked at D. L. Geary Brewing, in Portland, to learn the Pugsley/Austin system of ale brewing.

Kennebunkport has about 50 draft accounts around Maine. Future plans call for a limited bottling line to carry 22-oz. bottles for off-premise sales.

Taint Town Pale Ale: *British-style bitter*
Shipyard Export Ale
Capt. Eli's Kennebunk Porter
Goat Island Light
Fast Freddie's Ultra Light

1992:   **473 barrels** (opened in June)
1993:   **2,328 barrels**

LAKE ST. GEORGE BREWING
RR 1, Box 2505
Liberty, ME 04949   207-589-4180

Co-Owners: Kellon Thames and Dan McGovern
Brewers: Thames and McGovern
Equipment: 7-barrel system locally fabricated with used dairy equipment
Opened: June 1993

Lake St. George Brewery is somewhere between an advanced home-brewing system and a modest commercial operation. Its home location qualifies it as a home brewery; its 7-barrel size stretches to the lower rungs of commercial brewing.

Lake St. George Brewery is in McGovern's home overlooking the eponymous body of water in back of the house. Along with Sunday River Brewing in Bethel, it is the only Maine brewery not located on the tourist-traveled coastline. Brewing begins in a first-floor addition where the grain is milled, mashed and boiled, and the wort piped downstairs to the fermenters and storage vessels. All of their beer is kegged and sold to restaurants and taverns along Maine's Downeast coastline from Portland to Bar Harbor. Lake St. George was the state's eighth craft brewery when it opened in June 1993.

Both McGovern and Thames are keeping their day jobs while their brewery is in its infancy; McGovern is a meat cutter at a grocery store and Thames works for a graphics company.

Dirigo Ale: *a brown ale, the brewery's first offering*
Lake St. George Amber: *first brewed in December 1993*

1993:   52 barrels (opened in June)

 **SEA DOG BREWING**
43 Mechanic Street
Camden, ME 04843   207-236-6863

Co-owners: Pete & Cindy Camplin
Brewer: Dennis Hansen
Equipment: 7-barrel Peter Austin system
Opened: April 1993

Peter Camplin had been a homebrewer for 30 years and a general contractor for 22 years when he decided to combine his two talents. His 120-seat Sea Dog Brewpub is in the Knox Mill, one of the Maine's largest and oldest woolen mills. The mill overlooks the Megunticook River on the western shore of Penobscot Bay.

Sea Dog recognizes the achievement of Camplin's Great Pyrenees dog, Barney, who likes to sail, much like Camden's earlier generations of sailors and fishermen did.

Camplin hired Alan Pugsley, who developed two other Maine breweries, Geary and Kennebunkport. The Camplin family is all involved in the brewpub; Peter overseas brewing, wife Cindy manages the gift shop, son Peter is beverage manager, son Brett is chef, and daughter-in-law Karyn manages the restaurant.

Birch beer, root beer, and cream soda will be made for the busy tourist season. Seadog is the first lager brewery in Maine, but it will also brew English and Scottish-style ales. Future plans include distributing Seadog's beers to the local retail and tavern trade.

Brewpub fare: *New England seafood, stews, and chowders*

Penobscot Maine Lager
Windjammer Maine Ale
Old Baggywrinkle ESB
Rootin' Raspberry Belgian Lambic
Frosty Pumpkin Ale
Toasty Nut Maine Porter
Black Irish Maine Stout
Old East India Pale Ale
Old Gollywobbler Mild Brown Ale

1993:   N/A (opened in May)

SUGARLOAF BREWING
Sugarloaf, ME   207-237-2211

Co-owners: Jim McManus & Dick Leeman
Brewer:
Equipment: 14-barrel Peter Austin system
Opened: May 1994

Sugarloaf Brewing is on the access road to the popular ski resort where thousands of skiers come during Maine's long, snowy winter season. The brewery is in a new barn built to reflect the rural resort setting. During the summer, tourists come for golfing, rafting, fishing, and hiking. Sugarloaf is 2.5 hours north of Portland. The closest town is Kingfield, 15 miles away.

Carrabassett Pale Ale: *named after the local river which flows when it's not frozen.*

SUNDAY RIVER BREWING
One Sunday River Road
Bethel, ME 04217   207-824-3541

President: Grant Wilson
Brewer: Peter Leavitt
Equipment: 7-barrel JV Northwest system
Opened: December 18, 1992

The Sunday River ski resort is located in Bethel in the White Mountains northwest of Portland, along Route 26. Founders Grant Wilson and Peter Leavitt lived on the West Coast, where they developed a taste for craft beers. They believed Down Easters would have little problem adjusting to the full-tasting brews once they had the choice.

Sunday River opened December 1992 in time for the busy ski season, which attracts skiers from as far south as Boston and New York. In the summer, vacationers visit the resort for hiking, camping, and mountain biking. The brewpub also sells keg beer to Portland taverns. Capacity is 2,300 barrels/year.

Brewpub menu: *pubfare with seafood specialities*

Black Bear Porter
Pyrite Golden Ale
Mollyocket IPA
Sunday River Alt
Ragtop Amber Ale
Grand Trunk Eisbock
Brass Balls Barley Wine

1993:   1,100 barrels

50 Terminal Street
Boston, MA 02129   617-242-6464

Owners: Chris Lohring & Alex Reveliotty
Brewer: Al Marzi
Equipment: 20-barrel Peter Austin system
Opened: April 1994

Atlantic Coast is Boston's new craft brewery, the first to open since 1987. It opened in April 1994 in an old shipping warehouse in the Charlestown suburb of Boston. The brewery is on the Mystic River and the first brewery to pay taxes in Charlestown since the Commercial Brewery closed in 1940. Charlestown was also once home of the Van Nostrand Brewery, the largest bottled ale brewery in the 19th century. Before the turn of the century, Boston had 28 breweries and almost all brewed ales.

Founders Alex Reveliotty and Chris Lohring were two renegades from the mainstream world of computer consulting and nonprofit work. Reveliotty, 26, had lost his job in the computer industry and enrolled in the Central Massachusetts Entrepreneurial Center, organized to retrain the unemployed. After completing the course, Reveliotty raised more than $250,000 in 1993 to begin his brewing venture.

Chris Lohring, 28, also completed an entrepreneurs program at Northeastern University and worked at the Cambridge Community Services agency on youth programs. He had been a homebrewer for 5 years and apprenticed at Maine's Kennebunkport Brewery after he and Alex became partners. Lohring completed Austin & Partners brewing school to learn how to brew authentic English-style ales.

Reveliotty and Lohring wanted to stay in Boston and brew traditional ales like those brewed by Boston's old breweries. They were fortunate to find a site in a 5,000 sq. ft. warehouse in the Charlestown Commerce Center close to downtown, the Navy Yard, and Route 93, Route 1, the Southeast Expressway, and the Mass Pike.

Atlantic Coast will concentrate on brewing two draft ales, Tremont Ale and Tremont Best Bitter. They will distribute their cask-conditioned Tremont Best Bitter to local taverns and pubs. Cask-conditioned beers are

traditional in England but rare in the U.S. American pubs and taverns have, until recently, shied away from dispensing unfiltered, unpasteuized cask-conditioned ales because they are so perishable and must be drunk within a day or two to stay fresh. They require special handling as well as beer engines to dispense the ale without carbonation.

The name Tremont came from the three hills which John Winthrop saw when he settled in Charlestown and looked across the Charles River toward present-day Boston. He called it Trimountaine, which was later shortened to Tremont. It was Boston's original name.

Atlantic Coast publishes a little sheet, *Tremont Times*, about news from their new establishment. Its editorial style is chatty and goofy, like the more entertaining beer publications out there. Although everyone knows brewing is a serious, competitive business, it fortunately has its light side. After all, we're talking beer here, not brain surgery, thank God.

The winter issue mentioned the brewery's "Wall of Shame," recognizing brewing failures like Billy Beer, Zima Clear Malt, and dry beers. The column mentioned that space is being reserved for the ice beers which should show up on the shelf sometime soon.

Tremont Ale: *a classic English-style pale ale; copper colored, brewed with English malts and East Kent Goldings and Fuggles hops*

Tremont Best Bitter: *a cask-conditioned ale dry hopped with East Kent Golding hops*

 BOSTON BEER COMPANY/ SAMUEL ADAMS BREWERY
30 Germania Street
Boston, MA 02130   617-482-1332

President: Jim Koch
Brewer: Dave Grinnell in Boston; contract brewed at Pittsburgh Brewery in Pittsburgh, PA, Stroh Brewery in Lehigh Valley, PA, and Blitz-Weinhard Brewery in Portland, OR
Equipment: 25-barrel Pub brewing system
Opened: April 1985

Jim Koch's Boston Beer Company set the craft brewing world on fire when he went to the Great American Beer Festival in June 1985 as a first-time entrant. With a whirlwind of promotion, Koch's Samuel Adams Boston Lager won the consumer preference poll as the Best Beer in America, even though his beer had only just appeared in April in Boston markets. Koch subsequently won the consumer preference poll again in 1986 and 1987 amid heated controversy about convention floor politicking. Koch dropped out for a year, but won again in 1989. The festival sponsors dropped the controversial consumer preference poll in 1990

and substituted a blind professional tasting. The first year of the professional panel, Boston Lager won the gold medal in the European Pilsener
category.

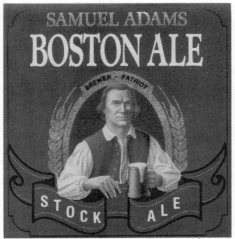

Koch was neither the first
contract brewer to make an
amber lager or to use Dr.
Joseph Owades as a brewing
consultant. New Amsterdam
Lager, Olde Heurich Amber
Lager, Brooklyn Lager, and a
few no longer in business (XIII
Colony, Great Lakes) have used
this same model of brewing at
a regional brewery with a professional brewing consultant.
This arrangement frees up the
owner to develop a market in a
region and promote the beer,
all without the cost or head-
aches of running an expensive and time-consuming brewery. Koch wasn't
the first to see the beauty and efficiency in contract brewing, just the
most successful.

Koch began by contract brewing his beer at Pittsburgh Brewery in
1985, following the example of Matthew Reich's brewing New Amsterdam
at the F. X. Matt Brewery in Utica, NY. When Koch wanted to sell beer on
the West Coast, he contracted with the Blitz-Weinhard Brewery in Portland, Oregon. When demand for his beer went through the roof, Koch
struck a third contract brewing arrangement with the Matt Brewery. He
left Matt in 1994 and went to the Stroh Brewery in Lehigh Valley, Pennsylvania which has much greater capacity to meet his future demand.

From first-year production of 7,000 barrels in 1985, Boston Beer has
grown almost 6,600% to 460,000 barrels in 1993. Koch's method has been
to use expensive targeted radio and print advertising and a team of sales
representatives in major markets. None of these efforts has come cheap.
The result of Koch's aggressive competition is phenomenal growth and a
product line that is nationally known. Koch may not have made friends
with his tactics, but he has taught brewers about developing a national
market for craft beers with an innovative product line and aggressive
competition.

In 1989, Koch opened a small brewery in a suburban Boston building
once occupied by the Haffenreffer Brewery. The Boston brewery produces
only a fraction of nationwide sales and is used mainly to brew test batches. But to counter opposition that he is only a contract brewer, Koch
brews one batch of each beer in Boston each year. Dave Grinnell is pro-

duction manager at the Boston Brewery and is in charge of day-to-day operations. Grinnell is a graduate of the Siebel Institute in Chicago and previously brewed at New Amsterdam Brewery in New York. He travels with Koch every year to England and Germany to sample the annual hop harvest and purchase hops for the next year.

Koch recently has escalated his national marketing efforts to bring the awareness of his beers to consumers who don't read beer publications or patronize brewpubs. He conducted a cross-merchandising campaign in 1993 with Pepperidge Farms during Christmas. He followed with a full-color 8-page advertorial spread in the *New York Times Sunday Magazine* on June 5, 1994. New ventures will include innovative scratch-and-sniff print ads in *Rolling Stone* and *Sports Illustrated.*

Critics may fault Koch's tactics, but few criticize him on the exceptionally high quality beers he brews. He has been one of the most determined to bring first-rate beers to the American marketplace. Walk into any restaurant, liquor store, or tavern, and if craft beers are available, Samuel Adams likely will be present. That placement did not come cheap or without creative marketing. Several have copied Koch's methods, but few have done it as well.

What Koch will do in the future is unknown. He will likely become the first million-barrel-a-year craft brewer by 1995. And despite numerous rumors, he has no intentions to sell out to a larger brewery even though Coors and Anheuser-Busch have reportedly had discussions with Koch. Koch says he's having too much fun to sell out.

Koch enjoys turning the beer world on its head. He does not seem willing to let someone else take over his show, even if he could become very wealthy in the process. The experience of watching Michael Jordan try to find joy in other pursuits cannot be lost on Koch. After winning three consecutive NBA titles, it has been painful to watch Jordan try to come up with a second act. After winning four "Best Beer in America" awards, it would be hard for Koch to find another Everest to climb.

Whatever Koch does will be watched carefully by readers of the *Wall Street Journal* and the legions of craft brewers. In July 1993, he appeared on the McNeil-Lehrer News Hour in a segment on international trade and the effect of excise taxes on exports of American beers. He also has been quoted extensively in major business journals which consider him the leading force in the industry. President Bill Clinton and his wife Hillary have even publicly stated they drink Samuel Adams.

In the near term, Boston Beer sales are likely to reach 720,000 barrels in 1994 and edge toward 1 million barrels the next year. The latest addition to Boston Beer's impressive portfolio of 12 beers will be a triple bock scheduled for roll-out in August 1994. The potent beer will come in at a certified 17.4% alcohol by weight, using three yeasts and aging in a winery. It will go into the Guinness Book of Records as the highest alcohol beer in the world. Brewer of the triple bock is Jose Ayala, a brewer from the Dominican Republic, who formerly brewed at the Bohemia brewery.

Samuel Adams Boston Lager: *amber lager with robust creamy head, powerful hop aroma and thick, luscious malty aftertaste. A truly distinctive and memorable beer that has set a standard for other craft brewers to meet; named Best Beer in America at 1985, 1986, 1987, and 1989 Great American Beer Festivals*

Boston Lightship: *winner of gold medal in American light pilsener category in 1988 Great American Beer Festival, bronze in 1989 GABF; brewed with one-third less malt producing a lower calorie beer*

Boston Ale: *brewed at Boston brewery with Kent Goldings and Fuggles hops; gold medal winner in ale category at 1989 GABF, silver in Dusseldorf alt style at 1991 GABF and gold in 1992 GABF*

Samuel Adams Double Bock: *brewed with more malt than any other beer in the U.S., over a half pound per bottle; a rich, full-bodied beer with a distinctive, malty aftertaste; gold medal winner in doppelbock category at 1990 GABF, silver medal winner in bock category at 1993 GABF*

Samuel Adams Octoberfest: *aged for two months, reddish amber, brewed with Halltertau and Tettnang hops; silver medal winner in amber lager category at 1993 GABF*

Samuel Adams Winter Lager: *a dark wheat bock; silver medal winner in German wheat category at 1992 GABF*

Samuel Adams Wheat: *brewed with malted wheat; Hallertau, Tettnang, and Saaz hops; silver medal winner in German wheat category at 1992 GABF*

Samuel Adams Cranberry Lambic: *brewed with wheat; a pale rose-color with a slight haze; very light fruit taste and a mildly tart aftertaste*

Samuel Adams Cream Stout: *a rich, mellow stout brewed with roasted chocolate malt and roasted unmalted barley; a superb and memorable cream stout that ranks as a world-class offering*

Samuel Adams Stock Ale: *gold medal winner in Dusseldorf altbier category at 1992 GABF*

Samuel Adams Honey Porter: *a dark ale with clover honey and molasses added; brewed with Fuggles and Goldings hops, two-row Munich malt*

1991:   163,000 barrels
1992:   273,000 barrels
1993:   450,000 barrels

BOSTON BEER WORKS/
 SLESAR BROTHERS BREWING
61 Brookline Avenue
Boston, MA 02215   617-56-2337

Co-owners: Joe & Steve Slesar, Marc Kadish
Brewer: Steve Slesar
Equipment: 16-barrel DME system
Opened: April 10,1992

Boston Beer Works opened on April 10, 1992, opening day for the Boston Red Sox who just happen to play ball across the street in Fenway Park. If there is anything that goes with baseball on a hot, summer afternoon, it's a cold one – particularly if it's made across the street. Bosox fans are some of the luckiest in the American League East (next to Baltimore Orioles fans who have the Wharf Rat Brewpub across from Camden Yards) and can have a fresh beer before the game, after the game, or between innings if the Sox are blowing them out (or suffering their painful, late-season slump).

Boston Beer Works operates under the name Slesar Brothers Brewing. Canadian-born Steve and Joe Slesar are the two brothers who started the business with Marc Kadish. Kadish owns the Sunset Grill and Tap in Allston which has one of the most extensive selections of craft beers in New England. Steve Slesar formerly brewed at Commonwealth Brewpub and Mass. Bay Brewing. He supervises the brewing at Boston Beer Works, while Kadish manages the restaurant side of the business.

Boston Beer Works was involved in a bit of unpleasantness when their opening in 1992 was followed by a million-dollar lawsuit filed by the Boston Beer Company owned by Jim Koch. Koch claimed a trademark infringement with the use of "Boston Beer" in the name of the brewpub. The judge ruled that the names were not too similar and that Koch did not have exclusive use of the words "Boston" and "Beer."

The interior of the 225-seat Boston Beer Works is spacious as a warehouse, which it used to be. There are two bars, one off to the left at the front, and a long curved bar at the back with plenty of room behind the stools for patrons to sit, stand, or sip and gaze about the spacious room. The copper and stainless steel brewery is part of the theater under lights and behind glass along the wall. Sacks of grain are stacked on the floor creating a neo-industrial appearance of part-time brewery, part-time manufacturing plant, and full-time saloon. High ceilings, industrial fixtures, blonde wood, and large, open booths offer patrons a comfortable place to mingle on game days. Not much intimacy, but this is baseball and beer, not candlelight and fresh flowers on the table.

On game days and nights, fans are lined up ten deep at the bar to quench their thirst and argue the merits or deficiencies of the Bosox, their opponents du jour, or the latest political scandal. But Boston Beer Works is more than a home-away-from-home for baseball fans – it's also a watering hole for students from nearby Boston University, Northeastern University, and several teaching hospitals.

Lining the walls are the colorful logos of the beers served at Boston Beer Works. In the summertime, Boston Red, Blueberry Ale, Fenway Pale Ale are prominent; in the fall and winter, Climax Winter Wheat, Beantown Nut Brown Ale, Great Pumpkin Ale, and Buckeye Oatmeal Stout are brought out. Boston Beer Works has some of the most colorful t-shirts of any Big East brewery: Bambino Ale, Boston Red, and Hercules Strong Ale are classic brewing art.

Boston Beer Works proves that it is possible for a large, urban brewpub to produce highly distinctive beers in a range of styles brewed to high standards of consistency and cleanliness. With more than a dozen beers on tap at all times, there's not a beer drinker imaginable who wouldn't find a couple that didn't meet his or her standards. Service at Boston Beer Works is also highly efficient and experienced. Annual brewing capacity is 3,000 barrels.

Brewpub Menu: *full range of lunches and dinners with seafood, Southwest cuisine, salads, burgers, and pastas*

Boston Beer Works Blueberry Ale: *served with fresh blueberries dropped into the glass; a golden ale with mild, pleasant taste of blueberries*
Boston Beer Works Raspberry Ale
Back Bay India Pale Ale
Boston Red
Bambino Ale
Fenway Pale Ale: *a crisp, pleasant, mildly hoppy ale*
Hercules Strong Ale: *a honey flavored ale with a pleasant, dry finish*
Kenmore Kolsch
Beantown Nut Brown Ale
Muddy River Porter: *a smooth chocolate flavored porter with a soft palate*
Eisbock: *a rich, doppelbock aged nine weeks to produce a malty tasting lager with aroma of clover and honey*

1992:   2,400 barrels (opened in April)
1993:   3,318 barrels

CAMBRIDGE BREWING
One Kendall Square, #100
Cambridge, MA 02139   617-494-1994

President: Phil Bannatyne
Brewers: Phil Bannatyne & Darryl Goss
Equipment: 10-barrel Pub Brewing System
Opened: May 1989

The Cambridge Brewpub is located in a century-old mill building that was converted into an office park with restaurants and shops. The building is a five-minute drive from the MIT campus and the high-tech corporate enclaves.

The 225-seat brewpub does a busy lunch and happy hour business that spills out onto the outdoor patio. The majority of its patrons are professionals who work and live nearby.

Cambridge won a gold for its Belgian Triple at the 1992 Great American Beer Festival, the only Boston brewpub to win an award. It has one of the highest production levels of East Coast brewpubs.

On one wall is a large mural depicting famous Bostonians from the Pilgrims to current patrons, employees, sports celebrities, politicians, artists, and local personalities. Senator Ted Kennedy is depicted as a ruddy faced, bloated lounge lizard chatting up a pretty young thing at the bar.

Brewpub menu: *seafood, complete dinners and lunches and pubfare burgers*

Regatta Golden: *a tart wheat beer with mild fruity aftertaste*
Tall Tale Pale Ale
Triple Threat: *gold medal winner at 1992 GABF*
Charles River Porter: *bronze medal winner at 1990 GABF*
Cambridge Amber: *ruby-colored with little hop aroma, mild nutty taste, and short finish; brewed with Willamette, Kent Goldings, and Galena hops*

1991:   **1,840 barrels**
1992:   **2,035 barrels**
1993:   **2,085 barrels**

CAPE COD BREWHOUSE
720 Main Street
Hyannis, MA 02601   508-775-4110

Owners: Robert Melley and John Cunningham
Brewer: Richard Young
Equipment: 7-barrel JV Northwest/DME system
Opened: July 1993

CAPE COD

BREW HOUSE

Robert Melley and John Cunningham had a combined 25 years of restaurant experience at the Cape before they opened their Cape Cod Brewhouse in July 1993. The site had housed several restaurants on Hyannis's Main Street; Melley and Cunningham converted it into a 220-seat Irish pub with appropriate Cape Cod nautical flourishes.

During the first year, Cape Cod's beers were brewed at Mass Bay Brewing in Boston.

Brewer Richard Young, who arrived in the spring of 1994, brewed several award winning beers while he was at the Seabright Brewery in Santa Cruz, California. Young's specialties were porter, India pale ale, and stout.

Brewpub menu: *seafood, pizza, salads, specialties*

Cape Cod Lighthouse Lager
Dakota Dark: *described as a hybrid of brown ale and porter*
Chatham Light
House Brew

1993: (opened in July)

COMMONWEALTH BREWING

138 Portland Street
Boston, MA 02114   617-523-8383

Co-owners: Joe and Lisa Quattrocchi
Brewer: Tod Mott
Equipment: 12-barrel English system
Opened: 1986

Commonwealth Brewing was the second urban brewpub in the Big East. Richard Wrigley, an English businessman was the first owner. He had earlier opened Manhattan Brewing in New York and later moved on to the Pacific Northwest Brewpub in Seattle. The original brewery had several features that made it difficult to operate as an efficient brewpub restaurant–square fermenters, a tiny kitchen directly behind the bar, and copper kettles that served only as ornaments in the bar serving area. Despite Commonwealth's early entry and its unique downtown location, it never reached its full potential.

In December 1992, Joe and Lisa Quattrocchi bought Commonwealth and began massive a overhaul of the operation. Joe had been a mortgage banker with Bankers Trust in New York, and Lisa was a lawyer who handled the family's real estate business. They believed they could develop a profitable operation and made several management changes to turn the business around. They hired Bill Goodwin, who had 20 years restaurant experience in Boston seafood houses, to serve as manager. They also hired Tod Mott, who earlier had brewed at Mass. Bay. They even came up with a formula for a contract bottled beer–Boston Burton Ale–brewed at Catamount in Vermont. The beer won the Best Ale in Boston in two local magazines in 1993. The overhaul seems to have been successful.

Boston is blessed with several superb brewpubs, each with an original idea. Commonwealth's claim is its proximity to Boston Garden a block away, where the Celtics and Bruins play to screaming fans 100 nights every fall and winter. Many of these rabid fans love a fresh beer before gametime – especially if it is brewed down the street. Game night routine at Commonwealth begins with a few fans dropping in about 5:00 PM for a couple of beers and a bite to eat. By 6:00, the place is filled to capacity of 250 with about 75% of them eating. They pour out at 7:15 for the game and an evening of cheering on the local heroes. By 7:30, it's safe for locals to come in for an unrushed dinner with all the noise down the street. But by 10:00 PM, the hungry and thirsty fans are back for some post-game celebration or commiseration. Cheers seems pretty tame compared to the action at Commonwealth.

One of the biggest events at Commonwealth during the winter is the annual Beanpot hockey tournament between Harvard, Boston College, Boston University, and MIT. During three nights in February, the Garden and Commonwealth are packed to the ceiling with screaming students and alumni who can't get enough of collegiate hockey and brewpub beer. Kind of makes one want to move to Boston just for this sort of silliness.

With the management changes, Commonwealth seems poised to become a profitable and popular Big East brewpub. A new Boston Garden is being built on the site and will be ready for occupancy in the fall of 1995. The new Garden will bring a schedule of 325 events per year including the Celtics, Bruins, and summer rock concerts. Construction is underway across the street for the new Suffulk County Courthouse. Between lawyers and judges stopping in for lunch, and basketball, hockey, and rock fans at night, Commonwealth is going to be a busy, busy place.

In addition to its regular line-up of beers, Commonwealth offers several drinks blended with their house beers: Snakebite – amber ale and hard apple cider; Gold and Lime – golden ale and lime juice; Black and Gold – golden ale and black currant juice; Shandy – Boston Burton Ale and lemon soda; Bitter Tops – Boston Burton Bitter and spritz of lemon soda.

Brewpub menu: *complete lunches and dinners*

Amber Ale
Boston's Best Burton Bitter: *pale ale, copper-colored, with medium body and pleasant, hoppy aftertaste*
Golden Ale: *medium-bodied ale with golden color and mild bitterness*
Porter: *medium-bodied, with hint of chocolate aftertaste*
Winter Solstice: *a spiced wassail with several spices added*

1991:   1,910 barrels
1992:   1,750 barrels
1993:   1,850 barrels

JOHN HARVARD'S BREW HOUSE
33 Dunster Street
Cambridge, MA 02138   617-868-3585

President: Grenville Byford and Gary Gut
Brewer: Tim Morse
Equipment: 14-barrel brewhouse
Opened: August 17, 1992

John Harvard's Brew House is about as tradition-laden an establishment that one could find in Boston. It's located on Harvard Square across from the campus of Harvard University, an institution stricken with serious pretensions of traditional academic correctness.

The brewpub is a replica of an English dining club with a menu running to hearty steaks, chops, sausages, ribs, English-style top fermented ales with a few traditional German lagers thrown in. John Harvard's traditional decor include worn carpeting, antique tables, exposed brick and granite, dark woods, and chandeliers. Stained glass windows covering one wall feature cultural figures from the 1960s and 1970s like Henry Kissinger and Richard Nixon.

Twelve colorful wooden panels on the walls created by local artist Josh Winer tell the fictitious story of John Harvard's life as a brewer in Boston in the 17th century. The murals chronicle Harvard's learning brewing from William Shakespeare before he left England to come to Massachusetts to establish a brewing institute in Cambridge. Someplace along the line, John Harvard was diverted and started up this little college named after him while the plans for the brewery never quite materialized. The irony is that Harvard University actually had a brewery on campus from the early 1700s to early 1800s to serve students living on campus. The brewery lasted until it became possible for students to buy beer at local breweries.

The spacious 10,000 sq. ft. brewpub seats 325 in five dining areas, a 63-seat bar, and private party room. The stainless steel brewery is located behind a glass partition behind the bar. John Harvard's staff was recruited from top restaurants and breweries: Sal Liotta was general manager at

Dakota's Restaurant in Boston, chef Joe Kubik was at Rowes Wharf Restaurant, and brewer Tim Morse was with Anchor Brewery in San Francisco.

Brewpub menu: *steaks, hickory-smoked ribs, sandwiches, burgers, salads, and soups with a British flair*

Cristal pilsner: *light golden in color,*
Bockbier: *sweet, malty pale bock with mild nose of alcohol*
New Town Light Ale: *blonde-colored, mild malty taste*
John Harvard's Pale Ale: *copper-colored, traditional British pale ale with mild malty taste*
Irish Export Stout

1992: N/A
1993: N/A

IPSWICH BREWING
25 Hayward Street
Ipswich, MA 01938   508-356-3329

President: Paul Sylva
Brewer: Jim Beauvais
Equipment: Self-designed and constructed from old dairy and fishery tanks
Opened: June 1992

Paul Sylva and Jim Beauvais started Ipswich Brewing in 1992 in an Ipswich warehouse. They used their own sweat to build the brewery with used vessels and tanks acquired from junkyards and local manufacturers.

Ipswich Ale is sold only on draft in Boston and northeast Massachusetts restaurants and taverns. A limited amount is sold in liquor stores in half-gallon jugs for the take-home trade. Old World Brewing is a joint venture with Ipswich and has purchased equipment for their combined use.

Ipswich Ale: *an unfiltered English-style ale*

1992: N/A (opened in June)
1993: 887 barrels

LOWELL BREWING
199 Cabot Street
Lowell, MA 01854   508-937-1200

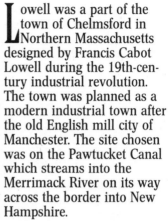

President: Guy Haas
Brewer: Paul McErlean
Equipment: 20-barrel Pub Brewing custom-designed system
Opened: May 1994

Lowell was a part of the town of Chelmsford in Northern Massachusetts designed by Francis Cabot Lowell during the 19th-century industrial revolution. The town was planned as a modern industrial town after the old English mill city of Manchester. The site chosen was on the Pawtucket Canal which streams into the Merrimack River on its way across the border into New Hampshire.

During New England's deep recession of the 1960–80s, Lowell went into a serious decline. Factory closings, high unemployment, bankruptcies, and crime all but destroyed the city. But recently, a revival has been putting new pride and industry into the town. The Lowell Brewery is part of the new face of Lowell. The brewery is located in one of the old mills.

Founder Guy Haas had been in the high-tech industry and visited California, where he discovered craft beers. He returned to the Lowell area and came up with his plan to attract investors in Lowell and bring a new industry back to town. He hired Will Kemper, a brewer who started the Thomas Kemper brewery in Poulsbo, Washington, and a consultant to several Big East breweries. Lowell's first beer is an American ale; a lager, a root beer, and specialties will follow. Distribution will be initially in northeastern Massachusetts.

Lowell began brewing in May, 1994. An adjoining restaurant, with a glass partition allowing patrons to look into the brewery, was one of the brewery's first accounts. Business will also benefit from a movie theater next door. Tours of the brewery cost $1 with the money going to the House of Hope charity for the homeless and battered women of Lowell.

Lowell's label is a colorful depiction of the town during the fall foliage season with rich autumn colors, the cascading Pawtucket Falls, and a brick mill building in the foreground. A true piece of brewing art.

Mill City Amber Ale

 MASS. BAY BREWING
306 Northern Avenue
Boston, MA 02210   617-574-9551

President: Richard Doyle
Brewer: Alan Marzi
Equipment: 20-barrel JV Northwest system
Opened: June 1987

Richard Doyle graduated from Harvard Business School with a love of beer that led him to start his own brewery. He and his investors raised $400,000 and incorporated, Mass. Bay Brewing in June, 1986 as Boston's first craft brewery in the city. They moved into their present site in March 1987, and their first Harpoon ale was delivered in June. By 1989, Mass. Bay had sold $1,000,000 in their second full year of operation.

Mass. Bay Brewing is located in the Marine Industrial Park across from the World Trade Center and Jimmy's Seafood Restaurant, a mile from Boston's financial district. The hospitality room is on the second floor where tours and tastings are held. A window looks down on the brewery floor allowing visitors to view brewing without crowding the workers.

Mass. Bay hired Nick Godfrey to take over marketing in 1990. Godfrey was the marketing inspiration behind the Smartfood campaign a few years ago, and he used his expertise to devise a grassroots marketing campaign. One of Godfrey's ideas was the 5:30 Club, a free tour and tasting for corporations or organizations after work. The program has been highly effective in spreading word-of-mouth interest in the brewery and spurring sales at local restaurants and taverns. Sales have been so steady for Mass. Bay, that during the long, snowy winter of 1994, when beer sales would be expected to slow down, production continued from January through March at summertime rates.

Another Godfrey initiative was new packaging which he designed on a Mac computer. The design retained the familiar diamond on the label, but added color and a flower or plant for each beer label (green and hops vines for stout, red and holly boughs for Winter Warmer, orange and fall leaves for Octoberfest). The labels are very attractive and appealing, inviting beer drinkers to get into the mood by savoring Mass. Bay's seasonal offering.

Mass. Bay is undergoing a major expansion with a 60-barrel brew kettle from DME fabricators and six 60-barrel fermenters that will triple their fermentation capacity. Draft beer is the only product at the Northern Avenue brewery but a new bottling line will be in place in 1994-95.

Mass. Bay's bottled beers are contract brewed at the Matt Brewery in Utica, NY. Approximately 45% of production is from their contract beers. Harpoon beers are sold throughout New England and south to D.C., Maryland, and Virginia.

Harpoon Ale: *brewed with Cascade hops; a light-bodied ale with a slightly dry finish*
Harpoon Dark: *described as a cross between a porter and a brown ale*
Harpoon Octoberfest
Harpoon IPA
Harpoon Winter Warmer: *a dark, spicy ale brewed with cinnamon and nutmeg.*
Golden Lager

1991:   **5,500 barrels**
1992:   **7,231 barrels**
1993:   **13,500 barrels**

 MIDDLESEX BREWING
   7 Crawford Road
   Burlington, MA 01803   508-452-9302

President/Brewer: Brian Frigulette
Equipment: 2-barrel Pierre Rajote system
Opened: January 1993

Brian Frigulette started his tiny craft brewery in 1993 in the basement of his house in Burlington. Frigulette was a serious homebrewer for five years before he made his decision to go commercial with a 2-barrel Canadian brewing operation. He works as an optician during the daytime and brews during the weekends.

Frigulette brews twice a week and sells his beer in kegs and 22 oz. bottles to local accounts.

Brown Ale
Oatmeal Stout
Golden Ale

1993:   123 barrels

 NORTHAMPTON BREWERY
(BREWSTER COURT PUB)
11 Brewster Court, P.O. Box 745
Northampton, MA 01061   413-584-9903

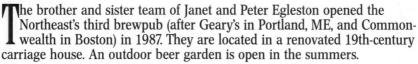

Co-owners: Janet and Peter Egleston
Brewers: Rich Quakenbush and Peter Egleston
Equipment: 10-barrel JV Northwest system
Opened: 1987

The brother and sister team of Janet and Peter Egleston opened the Northeast's third brewpub (after Geary's in Portland, ME, and Commonwealth in Boston) in 1987. They are located in a renovated 19th-century carriage house. An outdoor beer garden is open in the summers.

Northampton has a small off-premise business with 1/2 gallon glass growlers. Northampton's Golden and Old Brown Dog were chosen to accompany a U.S. Air Force friendship mission to Australia and New Zealand.

Since opening Northampton, the Eglestons have started the Portsmouth Brewpub in Portsmouth, New Hampshire and revived the old Jones Brewery into the Smuttynose Brewery, also in Portsmouth.

Brewpub menu: *full service restaurant*

Northampton Golden: *a pilsner*
Northampton Amber: *a Vienna-style lager*
Old Brown Dog: *a brown ale*
Black Cat Stout
Daniel Shay's Best Bitter
Hoover's Porter
Weizenheimer
Dunkelweizen
Smoked Brown Ale
Spring Bock

1991:   900 barrels
1992:   750 barrels
1993:   800 barrels

OLD HARBOR BREWING
25 Hayward Street
Ipswich, MA 01938   508-356-7779

Co-owners: Lou Amorati & John Munro
Brewer: John Munro
Equipment: Contract brewed at Ipswich Brewing
Opened: April 1993

Lou Amorati was an accountant for a Boston firm but was laid off when New England's economy soured in the 1980s. He got a job with the Ipswich Brewery on the Massachusetts North Shore and learned about the burgeoning craft brewing industry.

Amorati convinced Ipswich to let him make his own beer as a separate licensing operation of Ipswich. He agreed to buy two 15-barrel fermenters and a 7-barrel tank and began brewing his own beer before the new vessels arrived. Old Harbor's first offering, Pilgrim Ale, debuted at the same time as Plimoth Rock Ale, a contract beer made for the Plymouth Plantation.

Old Harbor's promotional literature has a drawing of Gov. William Bradford, whose often quoted diary entry aboard the Mayflower mentioned the reason for landing at Massachusetts, because, "our victuals being much spent, especially our beer." Pilgrim Ale is available on draft and in 22-oz. bottles in Boston-area taverns and restaurants.

Pilgrim Ale: *copper-colored pale ale brewed with 2-row pale, chocolate, and crystal malts and Northern Brewer and Cascade hops*

1993:   (opened in April)

OLD MARLBOROUGH BREWING
59 Fountain Street
Framingham, MA 01701   508-875-0990

President: Austin J. Moran
Brewer/Equipment: Contract brewed at Catamount
Brewery, VT
Opened: 1989

Austin J. Moran has a beer distributing company in Framingham and used his experience to brew his own beer on contract at Catamount Brewery in Vermont. Old Marlborough Brewing's sole beer, Post Road Ale, comes from the name of the colonial mail route between New York and Boston which was the country's first mail service. Taverns and coaching inns opened along the trail in the late 1600s, which became the village, towns, and cities of modern times.

Post Road Ale: *brewed with six-row crystal and carapils malt, Willamette and Cascade hops*

1991:   **1,108 barrels**
1992:   **1,650 barrels**
1993:   N/A

OLDE TIME BREWERS
197 Main Street
North Reading, MA 01864   508-664-2308

Co-owners: Richard and Jeanette Dugas
Brewer: Contract brewed at Oldenberg Brewery
Opened: 1992

Richard and Jeanette Dugas made their entry into the craft brewing industry when they introduced their Ironside Ale in 1992 in time for the arrival of the Tall Ships in Boston. Richard brewed a beer in the New England tradition of the ship captain's ale made from the first run of the mash, making a richer, tastier beer than that allotted to the common sailors. Prior to making the entry into commercial brewing, Richard was an electrician and veteran homebrewer.

In April 1993, Olde Time came out with 12-pack containers called "Dinghy Pack." The Dugases believe that consumers are not buying cases of beer as they did in the past and yet want more than the normal six-pack. The Dugases deliver Ironside Ale in a 1934 Ford truck that used to carry kegs of beer after Prohibition.

Ironside Ale is brewed at Oldenberg Brewery in Fort Mitchell, KY.

Ironside Ale: *an amber ale*

1992: 800 barrels
1993: 2,100 barrels

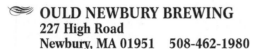 ## OULD NEWBURY BREWING
227 High Road
Newbury, MA 01951   508-462-1980

President: Joe & Pamela Rolfe
Brewer: Joe Rolfe
Equipment: Homebrew equipment
Opened: September 1992

The Ould Newbury Brewery is Joe and Pamela Rolfe's family operation. Joe is in charge of all the heavy lifting – brewing, bottling, distributing; Pamela handles the office work, accounting, and administrative tasks.

The Rolfes started their tiny brewery in the basement of their home where Joe had ardently pursued homebrewing for years. They started brewing commercially in the summer of 1992 and delivered to their first draft account, the Thirsty Whale in Newburyport, in September.

Ould Newbury's beer are available on draft to accounts in the Newbury area and in 22 oz. bottles. The Rolfes hope to move their brewery out of the basement and into a more spacious facility in the near future.

The colorful label on Ould Newbury's beers depicts a pastoral scene of the salt marshes of coastal New England. In earlier times, farmers would cut and stack the salt hay on cedar stilts called staddles to dry before feeding it to livestock. The label has a moody Van Gogh look to it without the heavy dabs of color.

Yankee Ale
Porter
Spiced Ale: *brewed with ginger, cloves, nutmeg, and cinnamon*

1992: (opened in September)
1993: **224 barrels**

MARTHA'S EXCHANGE BREWING
185 Main Street
Nashua, NH 03060   603-883-8781

Co-owners: Bill & Chris Fokas
Brewer: Dean Jones
Equipment: 7-barrel DME system
Opened: July 1993

185 Main Street, Nashua, New Hampshire

Martha's Exchange has been a Fokas family operation for more than 50 years, starting out as a luncheonette and candy store run by Mitch and Ethel Fokas. The family business has remained in the original building in downtown Nashua, the Merchant's Exchange Building, that dates from the 1800s. In 1988, the Fokas's sons, Bill and Chris, took over the business after they had completed college. They restored the building, converted the inside into a restaurant and lounge, and, in 1993, added a brewery.

The theme of the 240-seat Martha's Exchange is the 1920–30s Prohibition when organized crime ruled the cities, beer and liquor were made in bathtubs, gangsters shot it out with federal agents, and speakeasies were where the action was. The bar from Martha's reportedly came from one of Al Capone's Chicago speakeasies. Large bronze lights illuminating the brewpub once hung at New York's Grand Central Station. Half of one wall was a teller's window from a 19th-century bank.

The original brewpub equipment was capable of brewing 1,000 barrels a year. First-year demand was so great, additional fermenters were added in 1994 to increase capacity to 1500 barrels/year. Martha's Exchange also makes its own root beer. When brewer Dean Jones comes up with a specialty beer, the name is always the same – Specialty Hooch. Jones was a homebrewer who studied brewing at the Siebel Institute in Chicago.

Despite the success of the brewpub, a small candy store featuring homemade chocolates is still open at the front of the restaurant.

Brewpub menu: *complete lunches and dinners with several offerings prepared with beer*

Volstead '33 lager: *named after the act which created Prohibition in 1920*
White Mountain Wheat
Ale Capone IPA

Untouchable Scotch Ale
Bull Frog Stout

 OLD NUTFIELD BREWERY
22 Manchester Road, Route 28
Derry, NH 03038   603-432-3075

President: Jim Killeen
Brewer:
Equipment: 25-barrel Peter Austin system
Projected opening: Fall 1994

The Old Nutfield Brewery is another story of family entrepreneurship. Jim and Tina Killeen are using family financial resources, a state community development loan block grant, and a development corporation to open a small brewery in Derry. Killeen worked in the defense industry and served in the Marine Corps before starting his own business. Old Nutfield Brewing will hire about 10 New Hampshire veterans and handicapped to do its small part to lower the state's high unemployment rate.

Old Nutfield is calling itself "New Hampshire's Little Brewery," a title that could also be claimed by any of the other four craft breweries in the state. Derry was once known as Nutfield because of the butternut, chestnut, and walnut trees found by Irish immigrants who settled there in 1722. The town was renamed Londonderry after the city in Ireland where they came from. The town was later divided into separate towns of Derry, Londonderry, and Windham. Poet Robert Frost and astronaut Alan Shepard are from the area.

Old Nutfield's initial product will be Nutfield Premium Ale – "fire brewed with Irish attitude." The brewery will be located in an 8,000 sq. ft. former shoe factory in a shopping mall next to Wal-Mart. Artifacts from Old Nutfield's past will decorate the walls of the hospitality room when the brewery opens. Killeen eventually wants to open a brewpub on the site.

Nutfield Premium Ale

PORTSMOUTH BREWERY
56 Market Street
Portsmouth, NH 03801   603-431-1115

President: Janet Egleston
Brewers: Peter Egleston and Paul Murphy
Equipment: 7-barrel JV Northwest system
Opened: June 1991

Portsmouth Brewery is located in a renovated 19th-century mercantile building in the historical downtown area near the water-front. Around the corner is the courthouse with a bell tower and narrow streets crowded with tourists soaking up the atmosphere of a quaint old seaport. Portsmouth had a reputation as a rough Navy town from the 1960s to 1980s, when the port was busy with military activity. But it's a quieter time now, and most of the business in town is tied to tourism.

Co-founders and brother and sister, Janet and Peter Egleston, started their craft brewing ventures in Massachusetts in 1987 when they opened Northampton Brewpub. The venture worked, and the Eglestons looked around for another brewpub location before they settled on Portsmouth in 1991, where a restoration of the historic seaport was going on.

Peter was well known in New England homebrewing circles before he made the jump into commercial brewing. He was born in Pasadena, went to U.C. Berkeley for a year before moving to New York City in 1978, where he earned an M.Ed. at NYU. He taught English as a second language in Brooklyn where he began homebrewing. He credits good timing to his decision to leave teaching in the mid-1980s and get into the craft brewing business.

The Eglestons raised $1 million from investors and banks to start the Portsmouth brewpub. Even though the town is small and away from urban markets, craft beers are very popular with the tourists who stop in off Interstate 95 on their way to Maine. Peter says nearly every bar and tavern in the town carries craft beers. He credits the "ruthless marketing" of Samuel Adams for the widespread popularity of craft beers in the Northeast. Portsmouth's annual brewing capacity is 1,000 barrels.

Brewpub menu: *pubfare, burgers, seafood and salads*

Amber Lager: *most popular beer; Vienna-style lager*
Golden Lager: *pilsener brewed with two-row pale malt and Saaz hops*
Black Cat Stout: *an Irish-style dry stout*
Old Brown Dog: *a ruby red, sweet, malty brown ale; lighter than traditional Scottish ale*
Blonde Ale: *a flowery, hoppy aroma; slight honey tasting wheat beer*
Pale Ale

1991: **700 barrels**
1992: **1,043 barrels**
1993: **1,123 barrels**

 ## SEVEN BARREL BREWERY
Plainfield Road, Route 12 A
W. Lebanon, NH 03784   603-298-5566

President: Greg Noonan
Brewers: Greg Noonan and Mikal Redman
Equipment: 7-barrel self-designed system
Opened: April 20, 1994

reg Noonan knows a good thing. After running the very successful Vermont Brewpub in Burlington with his wife, Nancy, he was itching to try another venture to see if it would match the success of his first brewpub. His opportunity came when he discovered a location in Lebanon, New Hampshire, in the Upper Valley on the border with Vermont. Over the winter of 1993–94, he renovated a building and opened the Seven Barrel Brewpub in April.

The Upper Valley probably has the greatest concentration of rural craft breweries in the country: Catamount is a 5-minute drive to the south, Jasper Murdock's Alehouse and Norwich Inn is 10 minutes to the north, and Mountain Brewers is 20 minutes away in Bridgewater. Seven Barrel is also halfway between Noonan's Vermont Pub in Burlington and two brewpubs in Brattleboro, McNeill's and Windham. That puts Seven Barrel literally at the center of seven breweries, none more than an hour away.

New England has developed a strong beer culture that encourages beer lovers to travel to local breweries to sample the beers and meet others with the same devotion. The region attracts thousands of tourists every year who want to get away and live the rural lifestyle for a few days. Seven Barrel Brewery will be just one more reason for day-trippers to head north for a scenic brewery adventure.

The 120-seat Seven Barrel brewpub will have the capacity to brew 850 barrels a year. There likely will be little down time at the brewpub with a dozen ski resorts a half-hour drive away and numerous rivers for white water canoeing in the summer. Every Sunday from May to October, the parking lot across from Seven Barrel has one of the largest flea markets in New England.

Seven Barrel's traditional brewhouse includes a copper decoction kettle made in 1896. The brewery equipment is visible in the post-and-beam brewhouse tower in the front of the building, where patrons inside and the curious outside can observe brewing. The contemporary rustic interior features butternut wood paneling and an oak-paneled bar. Maxfield Parrish prints provide an artistic flourish. The painter lived and worked in a rural studio a few miles away.

All of Greg Noonan's beers are brewed with traditional ale yeast, Canadian and English malts, and American and English hops. Three beer engines planned for installation in the future will allow for cask-conditioned ales. All beers are served unfiltered and unpasteurized.

Brewpub menu: *American-style pubfare and traditional English pubfare specialities with Mulligan stew, bangers & mash, shepherd's pie, cornish pastie, toad-'n-the-hole, cock'a' leekie pie*

Old No. 7 Ale: *a pale ale*
New Dublin Brown Ale
IceRock Canadian Ale
Lickspigot Oatmeal Stout
Champion Reserve IPA
Sugarhouse Maple Ale: *brewed with pure maple sap, Canadian and English malts. and Mt. Hood hops; a golden ale with a mild maple aroma and aftertaste*
Wolf Roads Pilsener: *a European-style pilsener*

SMUTTYNOSE BREWING
225 Heritage Avenue
Portsmouth, NH 03801   603-436-4026

President: Peter & Janet Egleston, Paul Murphy
Brewers: Chuck Doughty and Paul Murphy
Equipment: 42-barrel brewhouse from Canada
Opened: June 1994

The Frank Jones Brewery was one of the largest ale breweries in New England during the 1880s. The brewery was founded in 1858 but finally went out of business in 1950. In the early 1990s, Don and Lea Ann Jones, who claimed a distant family relationship with the other Jones family, brought the brewery back to life with a contract-brewed Frank Jones beer from Catamount in Vermont. The Jones no doubt believed that with a craft brewing renaissance going on New England, you couldn't lose by rekindling a well-known brewery.

But the Jones's business went bankrupt in October 1993 after struggling with limited cash-flow, quality control, and distribution difficulties. The only asset left was the brewery equipment, including a 42-barrel brewhouse. The business was advertised as for sale at auction – and as occasionally happens in this very American industry – the Frank Jones Brewery was resurrected as the Smuttynose Brewery.

The new owners are Peter and Janet Egleston, whose credentials include Northampton Brewery in Massachusetts and Portsmouth Brewery across town from the Jones facility, and Paul Murphy, their brewer at Protsmouth Brewing.

Smuttynose is the name of an island off Portsmouth in the Isle of Shoals. According to local legend, Blackbeard buried treasure on the island when he was plundering the east coast in the 17th century. In the 1800s, a multiple murder took place on the island and a local vigilante mob found the suspect and hanged him.

Smuttynose Island is home to harbor seals and seabirds. An annual summer regatta features sailboats sailing around the island.

Smuttynose's bottles and draft beers will be sold in the Portsmouth area of seacost New Hampshire, southern Maine, and northern Massachusetts.

Old Brown Dog
Shoal's ESB
Black Cat Stout

UNION STATION BREWERY
36 Exchange Terrace
Providence, RI 02903   401-274-BREW

Co-owners: Joe Gately & Frank Hennessey
Brewer: Mark Hamon
Equipment: 10-barrel Czech brewery
Opened: December 28, 1993

Providence's Union Station Brewery opened in time for New Year's Eve, one of the biggest nights for restaurants. Located in the old depot which still provides Amtrak service, the 150-seat Union Station brewpub is a five-minute walk from the downtown Civic and Convention Center, Kennedy Plaza business center, and the State Capitol. It is Rhode Island's first brewery since Narragansett Brewery closed in 1982.

Founders and co-owners Joe Gately and Frank Hennessey came from corporate careers in the Boston area. Gately was in the high-tech field, while Hennessey worked for a major accounting firm in Boston. When they decided to get off the corporate ladder and start their own brewery, they chose Providence because of the availability of the Union Station location and the opportunity to be the state's first brewpub. The venture gained the support of the city, which provided a $125,000 loan from the Providence Economic Development Corporation. Mayor Vincent Cianci, Jr., attended the grand opening in December.

The ambiance is 19th-century saloon, with brass fixtures, exposed red brick walls, high ceilings and fans, dark wooden booths, and hand-painted cement floor. Photos and memorabilia from the old Narragansett Brewery hang on the walls.

Brewer Mark Hamon is a graduate of MIT and worked at two Boston brewpubs. He brews with yeast from the Narragansett strain stored at Chicago's Siebel Institute and cultured at the University of Rhode Island.

Brewpub menu: *seafood, gourmet pizzas, continental specialities, southern barbecue, and German pubfare*

Golden
Amber
Pale Ale
Porter

CATAMOUNT BREWING
58 South Main Street
White River Junction, VT 05001   802-296-2248

Co-owners: Stephen Mason, Alan Davis, and Stephen Israel
Brewer: Stephen Mason
Equipment: 28-barrel JV Northwest system
Opened: September 1986

The Catamount Brewery was a pioneer in the New England craft brewing industry when *Time* magazine discovered them in 1987 and published an essay praising their entrepreneurship and good beer. Marketing suddenly became a little easier, and Catamount overcame a significant obstacle all small businesses face – name recognition. Everyone, including editors at media conglomerates, love entrepreneurship.

Founder Stephen Mason started homebrewing at the University of Michigan in the 1970s. By the early 1980s, Mason was writing a business plan and visiting microbreweries in the U.S. and England, where he worked at Swannell's Brewery in Harfordshire.

When Mason returned to the U.S., he began looking at equipment and seeking financing. With a private stock offering and bank loan, Mason and two friends, Alan Davis and Stephen Israel, raised $230,000 through a private stock offering, $115,000 from a Small Business Administration loan, and $85,000 in a rural development grant. They built Catamount Brewing in a former Swift meat-packing plant in White River Junction on the Vermont-New Hampshire border.

Catamount grew approximately 20–30% per year beginning with 3,000 barrels/year capacity and building to 18,000 barrels/year in 1993. This expansion included a lucrative contract-brewing operation producing a range of well-respected beers for Seattle's Pike Place, Saratoga Brewing, Middlesex's, and Commonwealth's Brewpub. Contract brewing keeps Catamount's production schedules orderly during slow brewing times.

The brewery's logo is the wild eastern cougar (catamount, or cat-of-the-mountain) which once roamed Vermont's Green Mountains. The great cat is said to be extinct, even though rare sightings are periodically made.

Even though Catamount is in a remote area of Vermont, it attracts nearly 10,000 tourists every summer. White River Junction was a logging area but now draws river rafters, hikers, and tourists year round. Nearly 10% of business comes from the gift shop, which sells brewing paraphernalia, books, and beer. Expansion plans at the current location could take Catamount to 40,000 barrels a year.

Catamount Gold: *medium-bodied golden ale*
Catamount Amber: *a traditional English-style pale ale; well-balanced with smooth hoppy aftertaste*
Catamount Porter: *a dark, smooth chocolatey porter*
Ethan Allen Ale: *an English-style mild ale*
Christmas Ale: *the recipe varies each year; generally a well-hopped, dark, rich ale with an intense hop bouquet and aftertaste*

1991: 9,500 barrels
1992: 11,892 barrels
1993: 13,000 barrels

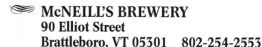 **McNEILL'S BREWERY**
90 Elliot Street
Brattleboro, VT 05301   802-254-2553

President: Holiday McNeill
Brewer: Reagin McNeill
Equipment: 4-barrel locally fabricated system
Opened: June 1991

McNeill's Brewery is located in the oldest firehouse in Vermont, built in 1820. The brewpub was designed and built at a cost of about $100,000 by Holiday and Reagin McNeill and opened in June 1991. Before they started the brewpub, Reagin owned McNeill's Ale House in Brattleboro.

Reagin brews with a locally made 4-barrel brewhouse in the pub's basement. According to local legend, the old Brattleboro jail house was in the basement of the firehouse where the brewery is today. The brewpub has an oak, mahogany, and wrought iron interior. Brewery capacity is about 300 barrels a year.

McNeill's serves 12 beers on tap at all times. Holiday McNeill is the sister of Alan Eames, the noted beer writer, who also lives in Brattleboro. Before he became a brewer, Reagin was a music student at Queens College in Manhattan.

Brewpub menu: *pubfare*

Munich Pilsener
Bohemian Pilsener
Big Nose Blond

Firehouse Pale
Dead Horse India Pale Ale
Slopbucket Brown
Duck's Breath Bitter

MOUNTAIN BREWERS
Marketplace at Bridgewater Mill, Route 4
Bridgewater, VT 05034   802-672-5011

President: Andy Pherson
Brewer: Bill Gault
Equipment: 15-barrel self-designed system
Opened: 1990

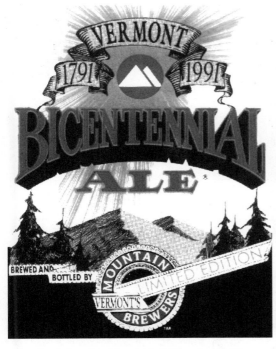

Andy Pherson was an electrical engineer working for a Boston software company and traveling to the West Coast, where he became acquainted with the craft brewing movement. In 1988 he got an idea of doing one in Vermont where he and his family vacationed. He eventually sold his home in Boston and moved to southern Vermont to start his ale-brewing brewery.

To choose his beer styles, Pherson traveled around the state and saw the popularity of Bass Ale. He went after the light-bodied, amber ale market, and in just three years had the third largest draft sales in Vermont.

Pherson designed and built the Mountain Brewer's system with Bill Gault and the backing of 10 additional investors. The brewery is in a roadside complex selling ski equipment in the winter and mountain biking, camping, and hiking equipment in the summer. The brewing equipment is downstairs and stretches almost the length of the building.

Mountain Brewer's growth has been nearly 200% per year since they opened in 1990; another 30-barrel fermenter, being installed in 1994, will take them to 21,000 barrels / year capacity.

All of their beer is sold in Vermont; distribution into western Massachusetts will likely follow when they satisfy the demand in their home state.

Long Trail Ale: *bronze medal winner in blonde ale category at 1992 Great American Beer Festival; medium-bodied, with slight dry aftertaste*
Long Trail Light: *silver medal winner in American lager-ale category at 1991 GABF; light color and light-bodied; 115 calories per bottle*
Long Trail Stout: *smooth chocolate taste with slight smoked finish*
Long Trail India Pale Ale

1991:   **3,600 barrels**
1992:   **7,000 barrels**
1993:   **12,134 barrels**

 NORWICH INN BREWING/
JASPER MURDOCK'S ALEHOUSE
Main Street, P.O. Box 908
Norwich, VT 05055   802-649-1143

President: Sally Wilson
Brewer: Tim Wilson
Equipment: 15-gallon Pico brewing system
Opened: May 1993

The Norwich Inn / Jasper Murdock's Alehouse is a brewpub – sort of. The Norwich Inn side of the house had been a coaching inn since 1797 and has a long and colorful history. It was the first tavern in Vermont to host a President when James Monroe stayed there and had dinner on July 22, 1817.

Jasper Murdock's brewpub was added in 1993 to serve specialty ales to customers. As one of New England's smallest brewpubs – 29 seats in the pub – Jasper Murdock's Alehouse has few pretensions to be much more than a modest brewing operation within a cozy coaching inn. Not a bad idea, come to think of it.

The marriage of an old coaching inn and modern brewpub is actually a man and wife operation with Sally Wilson owning the inn and Tim Wilson in charge of the alehouse. The two met when Tim was a Vermont banker with a foreclosed inn to get rid of and Sally appeared as a prospective buyer. The rest of the story could be told in a modern romance novel.

The original Jasper Murdock founded the coaching inn in Norwich in 1797. Although records are spotty, current residents would like to think that brewing was one of the activities of the inn, which would seem historically accurate. The original inn burned in 1889, but a Victorian-style inn was rebuilt on the site.

Norwich is a scant five miles up Interstate 91 from White River Junction, home of Catamount Brewing. The location makes it a popular stop, as it has been for nearly 200 years, for weary travelers or ale-searching adventurers. The inn has 21 guests rooms. With Catamount Brewery, Mountain Brewers, and Seven Barrel Brewery in Lebanon, NH, the Norwich Inn will offer weekend brewery package tours for tourists and beer lovers.

Tim Wilson bought a 15-gallon brewery system and brewed his first batch for about $2,000. He ferments in homebrewing-style glass carboys that are stored in corners and cabinets around the pub. But Wilson's beers have sold so well at the inn that he will have to expand in some way to meet the demand of summer tourists. He dispenses three beers at one time from the selection of a dozen beers he has brewed.

Brewpub menu: *appetizers, modest pubfare*
Norwich Inn menu: *complete breakfast, brunch, lunch, and dinner servings with seafood, game meats, and seasonal dishes*

Whistling Pig Red Ale: *an Irish-style red ale*
Jasper Murdock's Old Ale
Code Seasod Bild Ale
Old Slipperyskin India Pale Ale
Stackpole Porter
Short 'n' Stout
Fuggle & Barleycorn

1993:   35 barrels (opened in May)

OTTER CREEK BREWING
74 Exchange Street
Middlebury, VT 05753   802-388-0727

President / Brewer: Lawrence Miller
Equipment: 10-barrel system from Widmer Brewery
in Portland, Oregon
Opened: March 1991

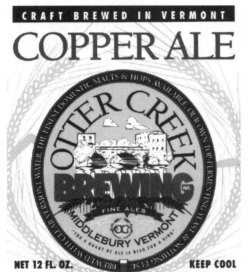

Otter Creek opened in March, 1991, in the picturesque college town of Middlebury in western Vermont. Founder Lawrence Miller was only 25 years old when he opened the brewery. He had grown up in New Jersey and was educated in Portland, Oregon, at Reed College where he discovered craft breweries. His academic field was neural physiology and psychopharmacology, the study of alcohol's effect on the brain.

Miller felt New England would be receptive to craft beers like those he found in Portland and the Northwest. He convinced his girlfriend, Ginger, to get married and move to Vermont with him. She took the challenge and today works for a computer software firm to keep the family's finances stable.

Otter Creek was started with $100,000 in family investments. The brewhouse came from the Widmer Brewery in Portland, one of the Northwest's first craft breweries noted for its German-style alt beers. Otter Creek's Copper Ale is an alt beer, and all of the beers are brewed with alt yeast. George Wehn, a brewer at Widmer and a friend of Miller's at Reed, made the trip and helped assemble the brewery and brew the first batches.

All of Otter Creek's beers are on draft. Miller plans to open a bottling line in the near future. In its current industrial park facility, Otter Creek could expand to more than 6,000 barrels/year capacity. Currently Otter Creek is sold only in Vermont.

Copper Ale: *the flagship beer; a medium bodied amber ale brewed with six malts, three hops; mild in flavor and aftertaste*
Hickory Switch Smoked Amber: *brewed with a small portion of malt smoked at the brewery*

Mud Bock Spring Ale: *a sweet, light ale*
Summer Wheat: *light bodied, with a citrus tang; brewed with 40% wheat, pale malt, and Cascade hops*
Stovepipe Porter

1991:   275 barrels
1992:   650 barrels
1993:   2,750 barrels

 VERMONT PUB AND BREWERY
144 College Street
Burlington, VT 05401   802-865-0500

President: Nancy Noonan
Brewer: Greg Noonan
Equipment: 14-barrel self-designed system
Opened: November 11, 1988

Greg Noonan is one of the most respected New England brewers. He is well known for his award-winning beers, the support he has given other regional brewers, and his leadership and vision in spreading the craft brewing influence around the country.

Greg and his wife, Nancy, started the 3,000 sq. ft. Vermont Pub and Brewery in 1988 after Greg had received national recognition for his homebrewing and writing. They moved to Vermont because Greg felt craft brewing would flourish in New England. More than a brewer, he was also a prophet. Noonan and fellow Vermont writer and homebrewer, Bill Mares, were instrumental in changing Vermont's law to allow brewpubs. Mares was a member of the Vermont legislature and the author of "Making Beer," published in 1984. Mares was also prophetic about the popularity of craft beers in New England.

When the 150-seat Vermont Pub and Brewery opened in downtown Burlington, it became known as an oasis for thirsty New England craft beer lovers. Many of the brewpub's most passionate and loyal customers come from the nearby University of Vermont campus and the Vermont state legislature.

Noonan is always on the cutting edge of brewing; he annually brews a Scotch Ale and Wee Heavy on January 1. The beer is tapped March 15 so consumers can enjoy the beers throughout Vermont's long winter, brief spring, and short summer. It gets cold and snowy for more months than residents like to acknowledge, so it's nice to have a comforting Scotch Ale or Wee Heavy to make the ordeal a little more bearable. It's one of the rewards of living in the north country. Greg's Auld Tartan Wee Heavy won a gold medal in the strong ale category at the 1993 Great American Beer Festival.

Both Greg and Nancy come from brewing and pub backgrounds: Nancy's uncles in Edinburgh were maltsters and barmen; Greg's great-great-grandfather emigrated from Ireland to Springfield, Massachusetts, where he worked in Hooker's Brewery.

Before opening the pub, Nancy worked as a substance abuse counselor. Now she counsels the staff on serving alcohol to the public responsibly. The Noonans are committed to responsible consumption; their motto, "All Things in Moderation," from *Poor Richard's Almanac*, is etched in the brewpub's glass door.

Greg has brewed more than 40 different beers since he opened. Some of the more intriguing beers are Joe Light, Divin' Duck, Frambrosia, Original Vermont Lager, Professor Doctor Flimflam's Porter, and Prohibition Ale. He was also one of the first pub brewers to come up with a recipe for a Belgian "white" beer, which he first brewed in 1993. Greg is a frequent speaker on the brewing circuit and has published numerous articles in homebrewing magazines and authored two books, *Brewing Lager Beer*, and *Scotch Ale*. His latest venture was opening the Seven Barrel Brewery next door in West Lebanon, New Hampshire, in April 1994.

Brewpub menu: *complete lunches and dinners with English and German pub specialties and assorted American selections*

Burly Irish Ale: *most popular beer; reddish-color, malty ale*
Brown Willie Lager: *Vienna-style, copper-colored lager*
Vermont Maple Ale: *dark, sweet ale for cold weather sipping*
Betelguise Weiss: *a sour-mash German wheat beer with a hint of cloves*
Dogbite Bitter: *assertive full-bodied ale with dark, almost ruby color and long hop finish*
Vermont Smoked Porter: *brewed with 120 lb. of smoked malt from a Geoff Larson of Alaskan Brewery recipe; a complex, smoked yet malty beer with delightful charred finish; bronze medal winner in smoke flavor category at 1992 Great American Beer Festival*
Auld Tartan Wee Heavy: *an intensely rich, high alcohol ale (9.6% by vol.) with definite sherry tones; gold medal winner in strong ale category at 1993 Great American Beer Festival*

1991:   700 barrels
1992:   847 barrels
1993:   855 barrels

WINDHAM BREWERY/LATCHIS GRILL
6 Flat Street
Brattleboro, VT 05301   802-254-4747

President: Spero Latchis
Brewer: John Korpita
Equipment: 7-barrel brewhouse designed by Greg Noonan
Opened: July 1991

The Windham Brewery is blessed by being a part of a family operation that saw a brewpub as an attractive and profitable addition to a downtown business. Spero Latchis, a Greek descended from immigrants, included the brewpub in his ambitious plan to bring life to a building that had been in the family's real estate portfolio for more than 50 years. Alan Eames, the noted beer writer who lives in Brattleboro, convinced Spero to consider a brewpub and provided artifacts and advice along the way.

The Windham Brewery / Latchis Grille is another example of a creative real estate / entrepreneurial venture. The operation includes a hotel, sandwich shop, brewery, brewpub, and theater. A bimonthly newsletter lists the activities of the diverse operation from movie schedules, menus, and stories about employees, to announcements of concerts and poetry readings in the theater, and new beers in the brewpub. A weekend in Brattleboro could find a couple never leaving the Latchis Hotel and having all their creature comforts accommodated. Another one of the joys of being a brewery adventurer!

The original Latchis Memorial Building was constructed in 1938 by Peter Latchis, Spero's father. His grandfather, Demetrius, had emigrated from Greece in 1901 and settled in Brattleboro. He started with fruit

stands, hotels, and movie theaters around Vermont that eventually included 15 theaters and hotels by the time he died. The building is listed in the National Register of Historic Places and is one of two Art Deco buildings in Vermont. Spero's wife, Elizabeth, runs the 30-room hotel that is part of the complex.

The Windham Brewery serves the downstairs 135-seat Latchis Grille which includes a bar, lounge, and two dining rooms. Brewer John Korpita was working as a carpenter on the hotel's renovation when he offered his homebrewing experience to Latchis. He got the job and brought in Greg Noonan of Burlington's Vermont Pub and Brewery to design a brewing system. The heart of the brewery is an old Campbell soup kettle and a mash tun from a milk holding tank. Korpita and Noonan designed and constructed a brewery that cost about $40,000, an incredibly low price for an operating brewpub system.

Brewpub menu: *Complete lunches and dinners with specialties from Morocco, Greece, Thailand, and the Southwest*

Whetstone Golden Lager: *named after the brook that flows by the brewpub; a light lager brewed with wheat, malt and 50 lb. of wildflower honey from a local beekeeper*
Ruby Brown Ale: *brewed with caramel, chocolate, and carapils malts and Kent Goldings and Willamette hops; a mild brown ale*
Moonbeam Pale Ale: *amber colored, mild, sweet malty taste with light hop aftertaste*
Blackberry Porter: *uses essence of blackberries; light berry aftertaste*

1991: 250 barrels
1992: 210 barrels
1993: 224 barrels

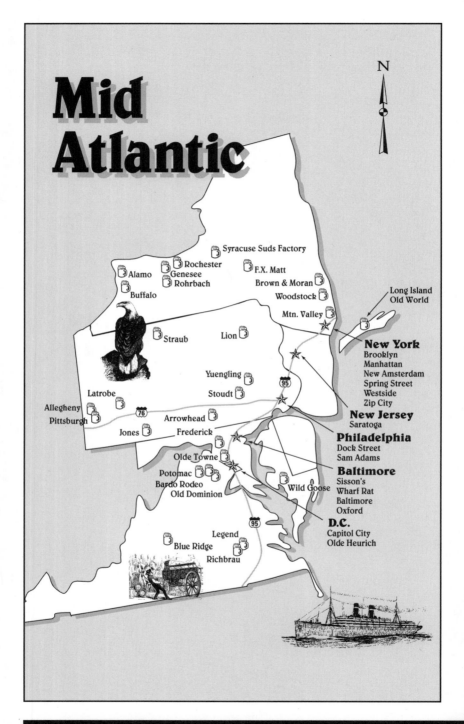

Mid Atlantic

N

Syracuse Suds Factory

Rochester
Alamo
Genesee
Rohrbach
Buffalo

F.X. Matt
Brown & Moran
Woodstock

Long Island
Old World

Mtn. Valley

Straub

Lion

New York
Brooklyn
Manhattan
New Amsterdam
Spring Street
Westside
Zip City

Yuengling

95

Latrobe
Stoudt

New Jersey
Saratoga

Allegheny
Pittsburgh

76

Arrowhead

Jones
Frederick

Philadelphia
Dock Street
Sam Adams

Olde Towne

Baltimore
Sisson's
Wharf Rat
Baltimore
Oxford

Potomac
Bardo Rodeo
Old Dominion

Wild Goose

D.C.
Capitol City
Olde Heurich

95

Legend
Blue Ridge
Richbrau

BALTIMORE BREWING
104 Albemarle Street
Baltimore, MD 21202   410-837-5000

President: Theo de Groen
Brewer: Bill Covaleski
Equipment: 17-barrel Schulz brewhouse from Germany/Mueller storage tanks
Opened: December 1989

Baltimore is a city loaded with tradition. From newspapers to ball teams to ethnic neighborhoods to local taverns, it is a city proud of its past and its ability to incorporate modern trends with local panache. H.L. Mencken, that professional Baltimore curmudgeon, never lost a chance to poke a hole in puffery and social "correctness."

This ability to forge ahead into contemporary times while hanging onto tradition has served Baltimore well. Its Inner Harbor renovation of the run-down, waterfront has been a major financial success. The Baltimore Orioles's move from old Memorial Stadium on 33rd Street to spanking new Camden Yards near Inner Harbor has been another fantastic windfall to the city. Three Baltimore breweries have also entered the new era of craft brewing by opening in a city that was once home to more than 20 breweries.

Baltimore Brewing, which opened in December 1989, may have the most authentic claim on the city's brewing tradition simply by its location. The brewpub is in a corner of downtown Brewery Park, the home of the Thomas Peters brewery, which opened in 1783. The site consisted of several buildings for brewing, cooperage or barrel making, and storing supplies and equipment. The foundations for several of those 18th-century buildings can still be seen in the park or from a patio of the brewpub.

Brewer and founder Theo de Groen comes from a background that is also steeped in tradition. De Groen is from the Netherlands, a country that has had many fine breweries. He graduated from the Weihenstephan Technical Institute in Munich in 1985 with a brewing engineering degree after five years of rigorous study. De Groen later earned an MBA from Duke and used his education and brewing experience to raise $1.5 million to renovate an old food warehouse near Fells Point, a popular destination with many Italian and Greek restaurants.

Baltimore Brewing's spacious brewpub setting resembles a German beer hall. The menu has a wide selection of German dishes, and all the beers are traditional German lagers. Baltimore Brewing's beers have become popular in a number of local restaurants for patrons who like to know they're getting the authentic "traditional" beer brewed in Baltimore.

Brewpub menu: *German (sauerbraten, bratwursts, schnitzel) and American style foods*

Helles: *traditional German pale lager*
Pils: *light color, medium bodied; brewed with Czechoslovakian Saaz hops*
Dunkles: *roasted malts are brewed to import a dark color and chocolatey tasting lager*

1991: 1,000 barrels
1992: 950 barrels
1993: 1,600 barrels

≋ FREDERICK BREWING
103 S. Carroll Street
Frederick, MD 21705   301-694-7899

Co-owners: Kevin Brannon & Marjorie McGinnis
Brewer: Steve Nordahl
Equipment: 15-barrel JV Northwest system
Opened: August 1993

Frederick Brewing is Maryland's newest brewery opening in historic Frederick north of Washington and west of Baltimore in the Cumberland Mountains. Frederick's first brewery was built in 1763 by John Charlton, who brewed for his brother's tavern next door, a common practice in the 18th and 19th centuries.

Co-founders Kevin Brannon and Marjorie McGinnis met when Brannon, a lawyer from Oregon, was in Maryland on business. Love blossomed, and they eventually decided to join forces in their personal lives (they married in 1991) and start a business. Brannon had been impressed with the craft brewing industry in the Northwest and used his experience as a corporate attorney to develop a business plan, find investors, and raise money.

After the Brannons's "merger," they raised $200,000 from a local bank with a guarantee from the Small Business Administration. They raised another $600,000 from investors and rented a 19th-century brick warehouse. They spent $100,000 on repairs and alterations before installing brewing equipment in 1993.

The Brannons met brewer Steve Nordahl at a craft brewing convention and hired him to brew for them. Nordahl is a graduate of University of California at Davis master brewers program. Before Blue Ridge could legally brew at their own brewery, they contracted at Frankenmuth Brewery in Michigan and Oxford Brewing outside Baltimore.

Frederick's original brewing capacity was 3,600 barrels, which increased to 5,200 by adding storage and fermentation tanks in January 1994. Sales have been so good in the Baltimore-Washington area that Blue Ridge expects to double production before the end of 1994 to take care of demand in Pennsylvania, Virginia, and Delaware.

Frederick brews four seasonal beers: a stout for St. Patrick's day, a ginger beer for summer, a hopfest for the fall, and a cranberry ale for the winter.

Blue Ridge Golden Ale
Amber Lager
Wheat Beer
Porter

1993:   **487 barrels** (opened in August)

〰 OLDE TOWNE TAVERN BREWING
22 East Diamond Avenue
Gaithersburg, MD 20877   301-948-4200

Owners: Bobby Solomon, Joe Kalish, Charles Covell
Brewer: Joe Kalish
Equipment: 7-barrel Pub Brewing system
Opened: May 1994

Olde Towne Tavern Brewery is suburban Maryland's first brewpub. The 300-seat tavern/brewery opened March 31, 1994, and but had to wait until May before receiving its brewing license from the Bureau of Tobacco, Firearms, and Alcohol.

The brewpub is in the J. A. Belt building, restored as a Victorian tavern, in old town Gaithersburg. Visionary city officials are hoping the Old Towne brewpub will breathe new life into a town which has been known mainly as a Washington bedroom community with few attractions to keep people close to home when spending their hard-earned money. Montgomery County officials put a limit of 2,000 barrels on Old Towne's production, a figure that could easily be exceeded if the brewpub has the success of many New England and West Coast brewpubs.

One of the owners, Charles Covell, was a developer who picked up the Belt building at auction in 1992 and wanted to do a unique restaurant.

The red brick Belt building was Gaithersburg's first building and is listed in the National Historic Register. The three floors will include a first-floor dining room and outdoor beer garden, a mezzanine-level dining room, and a combined dining area/museum with antique trains and photos on the wall. The owners spent $2 million to renovate the Belt building before opening.

The original owner, John Belt, built the building to sell dry goods at the turn of the century. After his business fell on hard times, it became a grocery store, post office, auto showroom, restaurant, photo shop, and, most recently, a pizza parlor.

Brewer Joe Kalish will supervise brewing at Olde Towne. He has more than two decades professional brewing experience, having put in time with Schlitz and Anheuser-Busch. He was one of the founders of Cambridge's Wild Goose Brewery on the Eastern Shore.

Olde Towne's Victorian theme includes a 28-foot mahogany bar, brass foot rails and fixtures, wooden stools at the bar, gold leaf, and green glass shades. The only things missing are bowler hats, spittoons, and bartenders wearing sleeve garters.

Brewpub menu: *complete lunches and dinners, seafood, steaks, and salads*

Forest Oak Amber Ale
Irvington Pale Ale
Log Towne Lager
Belt's Bitter
Diamond Stout
Windridge Light

🐟 OXFORD BREWING
611 G Hammonds Ferry Road
Linthicum, MD 21090   410-789-0003

President: Marianne O'Brien
Brewers: Tom Cizaukas & Drew Schmidt
Equipment: 14-barrel English system with Century tanks
Opened: 1992

Oxford Brewing was reborn in 1992 after the demise of the British Brewing Co., started in 1988 by English entrepreneur Craig Stuart-Paul. British Brewing fell on hard financial times, and the equipment was sold at auction in 1992 to Marianne O'Brien and her husband. The brewery was renamed and moved to an industrial park in Linthicum, a Baltimore bedroom community. The spacious facilities in the industrial warehouse will allow Oxford to add bottling lines or fermenters when expansion comes.

Despite British Brewing's financial problems, Oxford Real Ale remained a popular beer in the Baltimore and Washington area restaurants. Under new management, the beer's popularity enjoyed a resurgence in the mid-Atlantic states as one of the most traditional English-style ales on the market.

In 1994, Oxford began contract brewing Oxford Class at the F. X. Matt Brewery. Their bottled Oxford Class will be sold in the D.C., Virginia, and Maryland markets, and eventually throughout the mid-Atlantic states.

Oxford brews several beers for Washington and Baltimore restaurants. One of Capitol City Brewery's most popular beers is Oxford-brewed Eleanor's Amber Ale.

Oxford's Ales are served at three area baseball parks: Camden Yards for the Baltimore Orioles home games, Bowie for the Bay Socks, and Frederick for the Keys.

Oxford's Picadilly Porter: *a winter seasonal*
Oxford Class Amber Ale: *a traditional, medium-bodied pale ale brewed with British two-row pale and crystal malt*

Oxford's Real Ale: *a full-bodied ale brewed with Kent Goldings and Cascade hops; a pleasant hop "bite" and a fruity, complex taste with a dry finish*
Oxford's Raspberry-Wheat Ale: *a portion of frozen raspberries and 20% wheat produce a refreshing, raspberry-tinged ale with slightly reddish color and fruity aroma*
Oxford's Santa Class: *a dark, sweet holiday ale brewed with honey*
Oxford's Cherry Porter: *brewed with 175 lbs. of whole cherries*

1991:   3,000 barrels
1992:   3,100 barrels
1993:   N/A

SISSON'S/ SOUTH BALTIMORE BREWING

36 E. Cross Street
Baltimore, MD 21230   301-539-2093

President: Albert Sisson
Brewmaster: Hugh Sisson
Equipment: 7-barrel Pub Brewing system
Opened: September 1989

Baltimore has gone through impressive changes since the mid-1980s. The Inner Harbor Project revived the waterfront area with numerous shops, restaurants, and food kiosks. The relatively new National Aquarium attracted long lines of children of all ages to admire the impressive fish on display and the incredible shark tank. The Orioles moved downtown to Camden Yards in 1992 and drew more than 3 million fans the first season. Baltimore's a great city to live in or just visit – and we haven't even mentioned all the great restaurants.

The Sisson family traces its history in Baltimore back to 1803. The family owned a quarry and sculpted marble for Baltimore's Peabody Institute, City Hall, and the Washington Monument in D.C. A fifth generation of Baltimore's Sissons started a family restaurant in 1979 in Federal Hill near downtown and earned a loyal following of neighborhood patrons.

Hugh Sisson and his father were always looking for a new venture to get into and became enamored of the brewpub movement in the late 1980s. Hugh traveled to England and California to see first hand how these small breweries worked inside restaurants. The Sissons contacted Pub Brewing, who designed equipment to squeeze into their cozy 1,800 sq. ft. facility, and bought two adjoining storefronts to expand to 4,000 sq. ft. Brewing equipment was installed in the summer of 1989, and the Sisson's/South Baltimore Brewing Company became the city's first brewpub when it sold its first beer in September.

Sisson's is squeezed into a block next to a small grocery store, bars, and cafes. Across the street is the Cross Street Market where fresh produce, seafood and meats are sold daily. Sisson's consumers are neighborhood patrons and the beer lovers from the Baltimore-Washington area who don't mind traveling for some fresh beer.

Baltimore two other brewpubs – Baltimore Brewing and Oliver's at Camden Yards – are a 5-minute drive from Sisson's. Sisson's sells half-gallon growlers ($12.50 for the first container, $7.50 for refills), quarter and half kegs for off-premise sales.

Brewpub menu: *seafood, cajun and creole-style foods; specialties are blackened redfish, shrimp étouffeé, Bourbon St. Chicken*

Marble Golden Ale: *honors the Sisson family's career as stone cutters*
Stockade Amber Ale: *an old, traditional English-style bitters*
Stonecutter Stout
Gunga Din IPA
Prancer's Pride Holiday Ale: *available from Thanksgiving through December.*
Redweiser Raspberry Weizen
Cross Street Bluesberry

1991:   500 barrels
1992:   700 barrels
1993:   750 barrels

≋ WHARF RAT BREWERY
204-208 West Pratt Street
Baltimore, MD 21201   410-244-8900

President: Bill Oliver
Brewer: Howie Faircloth
Equipment: 7-barrel Peter Austin system
Opened: February 1993

Bill Oliver owned a popular bar in ethnic Fells Point called Oliver's, where he sold imported and craft brewed beers in the 1980s. When he wanted to open a brewpub, he found he didn't have the space, and the state bureaucrats said you could not have a brewing license and a liquor license. Bill had a simple solution: he turned Oliver's over to his son so he could open his brewpub.

Oliver found a promising site downtown on West Pratt with the Convention Center across the street and Inner Harbor a few blocks away. But when the city petitioned to move the Orioles into a new stadium at Camden Railroad Yards two blocks away, Oliver actually protested. He thought the 45,000 fans streaming onto Pratt Street for games would create too many traffic problems. Baseball fans drink beer, Bill. Before, during, and after games. That's America. It's what our Founding Fathers fought for.

Bill reconsidered when he crunched some numbers on his calculator and realized a few of those 45,000 fans would stop by the Wharf Rat Brewpub 80 times a year when the Orioles, who sell out most of their games, played. Opening Day came April 5, 1993, and Bill found patrons lined up at 6:00 AM even though the game didn't start for 8 hours! Play ball! Gimme a beer!

The second year the Orioles played at Camden Yards, the wise commissioners who bring us our national pastime faithfully every summer decided the All Star Game should be played in Baltimore. That night the Wharf Rat sold 4,000 pints of beer at $2.50 a pint. That translates into

$10,000 in beer tabs for a humid July evening. Still don't think that was a good idea to have a crummy old ball park in the neighborhood, Bill?

The Wharf Rat resembles a waterfront English pub complete with tap handles, beer engines, bar towels, seasoned wood, and Tiffany lamps. The exterior has the flavor of Merry Olde with black paint on the iron facade, pub sign, and lace curtains. The Wharf Rat's logo is one of the most attractive of any brewpub. It shows an old nautical scene with a three-masted ship off-loading barrels of beer at a dock. Beautiful.

Brewpub menu: *pubfare*

1993:   820 barrels (opened in February)

〜 WILD GOOSE BREWERY
20 Washington Street
Cambridge, MD 21613   410-221-1121

President: Jim Lutz
Brewer: Mark Scease
Equipment: 10-barrel Peter Austin system
Opened: October 1989

Brewing on Maryland's Eastern Shore across the Chesapeake Bay from the mainland began in the 1630s, when settlers landed and established the town of St. Mary's. The town had an alehouse by the 1660s to serve the sailors and settlers coming to the new colony. Today Maryland's Eastern Shore is more noted as a vacation land and food processing region. Frank Purdue's famous chickens call it home before they're dispatched to supermarkets and barbecue grills.

Canadian Geese wing down from the north in the fall on their way to warmer climes and spend a few weeks on the Eastern Shore fattening up on corn left in the fields. By the time the first snow falls, the geese attract hunters hunkered down in camouflaged stands and blinds. Geese are a major part of the Maryland economy – not the meat but the money left behind by the hunters who try to bag a few of the beautiful birds.

When John Byington and Ted Garrish started the brewery on the Eastern Shore, they chose the name Wild Goose for its strong allure to the region's lore. Cambridge is the county seat and frequent stop for goose hunters and summer vacationers on their way to Atlantic beaches of Rehoboth and Ocean City. The brewery is located in the old Phillips Packing Plant warehouse off Route 50. The 7,000 sq. ft. facility was once used to pack another Eastern Shore delicacy–oysters from Chesapeake Bay. World War II C-rations were also processed in the plant fifty years ago.

Alan Pugsley was hired to install Wild Goose's brewing operation and make English-style ales. Pugsley has installed and brewed at scores of breweries in England, Canada, and the United States. In addition to its own beers, Wild Goose brews house brands for regional restaurants. Brewer Mark Scease trained at Geary's Brewery in Portland, Maine, another Pugsley operation.

In 1992, Wild Goose was bought by a local businessman, Jim Lutz, who has grown the brewery considerably. Wild Goose's ales are distributed throughout Maryland, Virginia, and Washington, D.C., Pennsylvania, and Delaware. Under Lutz's management, Wild Goose has increased capacity to brew more than 10,000 barrels a year.

Wild Goose introduced two new beers in 1994, an India Pale Ale and Spring Wheat Ale. The wheat ale is the third seasonal beer after their popular Snow Goose Winter Ale and fall Wild Goose Porter.

Wild Goose Amber Ale: *the flagship ale brewed with Willamette, Hallertau, Tettnang, and Cascade hops; copper colored; light ale*
Samuel Middleton's Pale Ale
Wild Goose India Pale Ale: *brewed with two-row pale and crystal malts, Cascade, Willamette, Goldings, and Tettnang hops*
Wild Goose Spring Wheat Ale: *brewed with malted wheat, two-row pale and crystal malts, Saaz and Halltertau hops*
Snow Goose
Porter
Thomas Point Light

1991:   3,300 barrels
1992:   4,036 barrels
1993:   6,500 barrels

SARATOGA BREWING
412 Tenafly Road
Englewood, NJ 07631   201-568-0716

President: Chuck Schroeder
Brewer: Fred Lang
Equipment: Contract brewed at Catamount Brewery, Vermont
Opened: October 1991

Chuck Schroeder had his own advertising agency and at one time promoted two breweries, Stroh and Miller. He dabbled in homebrewing and wanted to get into the brewing industry. Schroeder eventually struck a deal with William Newman, brewer of Albany Amber, in New York. The two of them came up with a new product called Saratoga Lager, a Dortmunder-style lager. Schroeder worked on the packaging and promotion and hired former F. X. Matt brewer, Fred Lang, to brew for him. The beer was brewed at the Catamount Brewery in Vermont and sold in central New York, Connecticut, and New Jersey, where Schroeder lives.

Schroeder and Newman had a falling out and had to resort to lawyers to clear ownership of the brand name and label. Schroeder won out and had Newman's name removed from the label.

Saratoga Lager is a Dortmunder-style lager which Schroeder believes will please the American palate not accustomed to heavily hopped beers. He discovered the beer style while he was traveling in Germany working on a Lufthansa advertising account.

Saratoga Lager: *Dortmunder-style lager brewed with pale and caramel malt, German Hersbrucker, Hallertau Mittelfruh and Czechoslovakian Saaz hops*

1992: N/A
1993: N/A

BROOKLYN BREWERY
118 North 11th St.
Brooklyn, NY 11211   718-486-7422

Co-owners: Stephen Hindy & Tom Potter
Brewer: William Moeller
Equipment: Contract brewed at F. X. Matt Brewery, Utica, NY
Opened: 1988

Brooklyn Brewery is the first brewery to open in a borough that boasted some 50 breweries before Prohibition. The new brewery on the block's (or the borough's) first offering is, according to literature, a pre-Prohibition-style lager, whatever that means.

Stephen Hindy was a journalist working for AP in the Middle East at a time when being a foreign correspondent was a romantic and exciting profession. But with Middle East politics becoming a messy affair the last few years, Hindy felt it was time for a career change. He was replaced in Beirut by Terry Anderson, who was kidnaped by Islamic fundamentalists and held hostage for six years. Hindy was back in New York by this time, working for *Newsday* as a foreign editor and writing a business plan for a brewery.

Hindy and his partner, Tom Potter, a vice president at Chemical Bank, had both dabbled in homebrewing and were steeped in Brooklyn's brewing tradition. With a brewing renaissance going on in the country, and living in a city of more than 2 million people who remembered the city's old breweries, it didn't take much to see that a new brewery in Brooklyn would be a marketing dream. Potter and Hindy raised $500,000 from family and friends and hired Bill Moeller, who had been brewmaster at Philadelphia's Ortleib and Schmidt breweries. Although Moeller was retired, he was enticed by becoming a brewer in the town where his grandfather had brewed before Prohibition. Tradition. Nostalgia. Renaissance. Beer. As American as baseball in summertime–which Brooklyn knows something about.

The brewery's logo is a scripted letter "B" from the uniform of the Brooklyn Dodgers, who left Flatbush in 1957 for the earthquakes, fires, and mudslides of Southern California. When Brooklyn Lager won a gold medal at the 1992 Great American Beer Festival, Hindy put out a press release announcing it was the first national champion Brooklyn had had since the Dodgers won the 1955 World Series.

Brooklyn is a state of mind for many Americans. Between the Dodgers and the Bridge, the image of Brooklyn is redolent of middle class work ethic and local pride, with a touch of dark humor. Archie Bunker may not have lived in Brooklyn, but his cousins are still around. And they drink beer and talk about the old days when Brooklyn had a brewery on almost every block and a baseball team they lovingly called the "Bums."

Hindy and Potter eventually want to have a brewery at home and have looked at the old Red Hook area of waterfront warehouses and docks. A smart businessman might come up with an idea to bring a baseball team back to town so we can live the '50s all over again. Might as well bring back the Edsel, too.

Brooklyn's two beers are sold in the Big East and overseas in Japan, Thailand, Britain, Germany, Italy, and France. Japanese restaurants reportedly air ship cases to Tokyo restaurants and clubs for a touch of the real America.

Brooklyn Lager: *brewed with two-row Clagus and crystal malt and dry hopped with Hallertau hops; gold medal winner in amber lager at 1992 Great American Beer Festival*

Brooklyn Brown Pale Ale: *a bronze medal winner in brown ale at the 1992 GABF*

1991: 8,400 barrels
1992: 9,200 barrels
1993: 10,200 barrels

 ## BROWN & MORAN BREWING
417-419 River Street
Troy, NY 12180   518-273-2337

Owners: Peter Lindley, Gary Brown, Jim Moran
Brewer: Gary Brown
Equipment: 15-barrel Canadian system
Opened: February 26, 1993

Troy is one of the great historic cities of New York's capital region around Albany. The town was an active mercantile area in the 18th century and an industrial hub in the 19th century. Local manufacturers made square nails, industrial shirt collars, men's shirts, and throwaway collars. The *Monitor*, the Union's submarine that saw brief action during the Civil War, was built here in the 1860s. The first clothing union was organized in Troy, and it was the home of merchant Sam Wilson, whose caricature became known as Uncle Sam. Today Troy is more well-known for being the home of Rennsselaer Polytechnic Institute, located on the top of a hill over looking the town and the Hudson River valley.

During the Industrial Revolution, Troy was home to 22 breweries, including Fitzgerald, Quandt, Conway, Stanton, and Isengart. The second-floor walls of Brown and Moran's Brewpub has murals of these old breweries. Another eye-catching mural depicts a flowing field of grain with the title, "Brew It and They Will Come." Hidden in the barley is a baseball. A mural above the brewery shows the owners and employees dressed in 19th-century working clothes. Local artist Kevin Clark created the murals.

Co-owners Lindley, Brown, and Moran are all local businessmen who went to the West Coast where they watched the craft brewing movement come of age in the 1980s. They returned to Troy with visions of hops in their dreams and bought a century-old building for $66,000. They went to work renovating it, added a kitchen and room for a brewery, and raised money for their brewpub.

Brown & Moran's brewery is in a back corner where floors were removed to allow the equipment to extend from the basement to the second floor. The tower design makes brewing operations more efficient for the brewing crew. Patrons can watch brewing going on through glass partitions. The Brown and Moran 11,600 sq. ft. brewpub is in a former industrial area near downtown. An outdoor patio looks out on the Hudson River less than 100 yards away.

Brewpub menu: *pubfare*

Adirondack Golden Ale
Harwood's Porter
Sequoia Amber
Belgian Cherry
Weizen
St. Nick's Nectar

1993:   954 barrels (opened in February)

**BUFFALO BREWING/
ALAMO BREWPUB**
1830 Abbott Road
Lackawanna, NY 14218   716-824-8711

President: Kevin Townsell
Brewer: Fred Lang
Equipment: 50-barrel German brewhouse
Opened: 1990

The Buffalo Brewing Company is the mothership of the brewing operations that include two brewpubs in Williamsville and Rochester. Kevin Townsell started all of the breweries, beginning with the Buffalo Brewery in 1986.

Townsell took over the old John's Flaming Hearth restaurant in Lackawanna, south of Buffalo, to build the Buffalo Brewery in 1990. An all-copper 50-barrel brewhouse was shipped over from Germany. Fermentation and storage tanks, bottling, and kegging equipment were purchased in the U.S. and Canada.

The Abbott Square Brewpub co-located with Buffalo Brewing is a western-style bar that features country music, cowboy dancing, and Texas-style barbecue. Cowboy hats and engraved belt buckles take over on weekends. After all, Buffalo is closer to Wyoming than any other place in New York. Capacity at Abbott Square is 2,500, or about half the size of Laramie.

Brewer Fred Lang brews traditional German lager beers from barley and wheat malt imported from Bavaria. Yeast is imported from the Weihenstephan Brewing Institute, and hops are from German types imported or grown in North America. Buffalo's pasteurized lager is brewed at the F. X. Matt Brewery in Utica for distribution throughout western New York and select Big East markets –Washington, New York City, Boston, Atlanta, and Pittsburgh.

Townsell is in the midst of a major expansion and is raising $1 million by selling 200,000 shares of stock at $5 each. The expansion will include a new bottling line, grain-handling equipment, and storage tanks that will increase capacity from 7,000 barrels/year to 21,000 barrels. A new brewpub in Buffalo is also in the plans.

In the 19th century, when Buffalo was a major industrial city, it was the home of 35 breweries.

Brewpub menu: *barbecue and burgers*

Buffalo Lager: *a German helles light lager*
Buffalo Pils
Buffalo Weisse: *brewed with 52% wheat malt*
Blizzard Bock: *brewed to commemorate the "Blizzard of 1985," when 33 inches fell on Buffalo during one blizzard*
Paddy's Porter
Limericks Irish Red Ale
Oktoberfest Lager: *a Maerzen style brewed for sale in September and October*
Lang's Holiday Cheer: *an English-style Wassail spiced with cinnamon and nutmeg*

1991: 5,100 barrels
1992: 6,500 barrels
1993: 5,950 barrels

 BUFFALO BREWING
6861 Main Street at Transit Road
Williamsville, NY 14221   716-632-0552

President: Kevin Townsell
Brewer: Keith Morgan
Equipment: 10-barrel Continental system
Opened: 1986

The Buffalo Brewpub was one of New York's first brewpubs when it opened in 1986. Buffalo Brewpub was the first brewery in the city to open since the William Simon brewery had closed in 1972.

Buffalo Brewing has sister operations with the Rochester Brewpub in Henrietta and the Buffalo Brewing Company, which produces bottles and draft beer for off-premise trade. Kevin Townsell, a local restaurateur, started all of the Buffalo-area operations and is looking at opening more brewpubs in Niagara Falls, Ithaca, and Syracuse.

Brewpub menu: *pubfare*

Buffalo Lager
Buffalo Pils
Buffalo Wiesse
Limericks Irish Red Ale

1991:   450 barrels
1992:   450 barrels
1993:   475 barrels

 GENESEE BREWING
445 St. Paul Street
Rochester, NY 14605   716-546-1030

President: Ted Wehle
Brewer: Gary Geminn
Equipment: 1,000 barrel American system
Opened: 1878

Genesee Brewing is one of two New York regional breweries to have survived Prohibition and the mergers/consolidations of the postwar years. With more than 110 years of brewing in Rochester, Genesee is the largest family regional brewery and ranks as the 7th largest producing brewery in the country.

The brewery is located on a plateau overlooking the Genesee River that runs alongside Rochester. Genesee's founder, Louis Wehle, started the brewery in 1878, when virtually every town in New York had a local brewery.

Genesee is distributed in 24 states and Ontario. Three subsidiaries operating at Genesee are: Fred Koch Brewery, Shea's Brewery, and Dundee's Brewery.

Genesee Beer: *first introduced in 1878; brewed with six-row barley, corn grits, and Yakima Valley hops*
Genny Light Beer
Genesee Cream Ale: *top fermented and krausened to increase carbonation before bottling; introduced in 1960; silver medal winner in cream ale*

category at 1993 Great American Beer Festival

12 Horse Ale: *a light-bodied American ale brewed with six-row barley, corn grits, and Yakima Valley hops, and top-fermenting ale yeast*

Genesee NA: *(Non-Alcoholic)*

Genesee Bock Beer: *released every January in limited supplies; introduced in 1878*

Genny Ice Beer: *introduced in 1993*

Koch's Golden Anniversary Beer

Koch's Golden Anniversary Light

Michael Shea's Irish Amber

Michael Shea's Black and Tan: *a blend of porter and lager; introduced in 1993*

JW Dundee's Honey Brown Lager: *a mead; brewed with barley, Nugget hops, and Manitoba clover honey*

1991: 2,200,000 barrels
1992: 2,108,000 barrels
1993: 2,150,000 barrels

LONG ISLAND BREWING
111 Jerico Turnpike
Jerico, NY 11753   516-334-BREW

President: Dave Glicker
Brewer: Mark Burford
Equipment: 10-barrel Bohemian system
Opened: October 1994

The Long Island Brewing Company is scheduled to open during the fall of 1994 as the first or second brewery to come to the heavily populated island. Founder Dave Glicker has years of restaurant experience on Long Island and is convinced the area will go big time for local brewpubs. He is converting his Forty West nightclub into the brewpub.

Brewer Mark Burford was a home brewer and trained at Zip City and Mountain Valley Brewpub in Suffern. He is planning on brewing a combination of German-style lagers and English-style ales to complement the brewpub menu.

The brewpub is located in a strip mall with restaurants and retail stores off Exit 40 West on the Long Island Expressway. The second-floor beer garden will have climbing hop vines providing shade for summer patrons.

Brewpub menu: *pubfare*

 ## MANHATTAN BREWERY
40-42 Thompson Street
New York City, NY 10013   212-925-1515

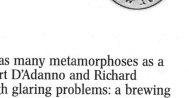

President: Group of investors
Brewer: Garrett Oliver
Equipment: 7-barrel British system
Opened: 1985

Manhattan Brewing has gone through as many metamorphoses as a cicada. First opened in 1986 by Robert D'Adanno and Richard Wrigley, the brewpub suffered through glaring problems: a brewing system never designed to work; a cumbersome Con Edison substation resistant to renovation into a restaurant, inconsistent brewing, and inexperienced management. The brewpub opened, closed, tried a spot of contract brewing, but never made it all work.

A group of Manhattan investors organized as Soho Suds, Inc., revived Manhattan Brewing and reopened in May 18, 1993. The touches of British pub have been toned down to appeal to neighbors who prefer, an American saloon atmosphere. A full-color mural, art deco black and white photos, and metal sculptures adorn the walls, making the brewpub more like a trendy loft gallery.

Brewer Garrett Oliver's career at Manhattan Brewing goes back to the early days when Mark Witty of Whitbread started the brewing operation. Oliver has links to the British CAMRA group and lectures on real ale in America. His research has taken him to the New York City Library where he uncovered old recipes for ales brewed in Colonial New York. He writes for several brewing journals and is a frequent speaker at brewing conventions.

Brewpub menu: *pubfare, salads, pizzas*

Weizen: *a spicy, floral aroma of cloves and bubble gum finishes with a dry, clean taste; brewed with Cascade and Willamette hops*
India Pale Ale: *derived from a 17th-century recipe; brewed with British Goldings and Fuggles hops; a clean, round hoppy ale without the characteristic sharp IPA finish*
Holiday Ale: *brewed with nutmeg, dates, honey, and cinnamon; spicy aroma with complex but pleasant spice flavors; a dry, mild finish*
Imperial Stout: *heavy, rich chocolate taste, sweet aftertaste*

1993:   N/A (reopened in May)

F. X. MATT BREWING
811 Edward Street
Utica, NY 13502   315-732-3181

President: Nicholas Matt
Brewer: F. X. Matt II
Equipment: 600-barrel brewhouse
Opened: 1888

The F. X. Matt Brewery is one of the few remaining family breweries still operating in the U.S. It was founded by F. X. Matt I, who learned brewing at the Duke of Baden Brewery in Rothaus, Germany, before he emigrated to America in 1878. Matt worked for the Bierbauer's Columbia Brewery, one of Utica's 12 breweries, until he founded the West End Brewery in 1888.

When the Matt brewery was facing declining sales and fierce competition from national brands in the 1980s, it discovered a niche in the brewing industry – enthusiastic entrepreneurs who wanted to make a craft beer but didn't have the capital to build their own brewery. Matthew Reich, founder of New Amsterdam Brewery in New York, began brewing his first beer on contract at Matt's in the early 1980s and selling it to upscale Manhattan taverns and restaurants.

Reich's contract brewing experiment worked amazingly well until he made a fatal mistake – building his own brewery and restaurant in Manhattan. The venture failed and Reich was forced to sell his share in the company. But the example of contract brewing at a regional brewery was not missed by other aspiring craft brewers – Jim Koch at Boston Beer (who started at Pittsburgh Brewery), Gary Heurich at Olde Heurich (Washington, D.C.) , Jeff Ware at Dock Street (Philadelphia), and many others who followed in their footsteps. Today Matt brews the well-known Big East beers, including Saratoga Lager, New Amsterdam, Olde Heurich, Dock Street Oxford Class, Brooklyn Lager, Harpoon Ale, and Prior Double Bock.

Contract brewing likely saved the Matt Brewery from going the way of countless regionals which didn't have a large enough market for their own beers. In the end, contract brewing is a novel and profitable enterprise for both the regional brewer and the craft brewing marketer. It's the better mousetrap approach to becoming a "brewer" without a brewery.

The Matt brewery has had four presidents from the family in its 106-year history: F. X. Matt I, who died at the age of 99 in 1958 (he retired in 1951); son Walter, who served from 1951 to 1980; F. X. Matt II, who was president from 1980 to 1989 when the Matt family descendants purchased the controlling stock from a family trust and shareholders; and Nicholas Matt, who was named president in 1989.

The most popular place in the Matt brewery is the 1888 Victorian tavern which serves as the gift shop and tasting room. Old brewery advertisements, Tiffany lamps, and Victorian-style bric-a-brac recall the old days when saloons, sleeve garters, handlebar mustaches, and women's feathered hats were the fashion.

The current Matt brewery with its 600-barrel brewhouse was built in downtown Utica in 1948. The brewery created the Birch Hill Beverage Company in 1992 to sell its non-alcoholic Freeport USA drink and a grain-based carbonated soft drink called Barlee Farms.

Saranac Adirondack Lager: *gold medal at 1991 Great American Festival in premium lager category*
Matt's Premium: *gold medal at 1984 Great American Beer Festival in pilsener category*
Utica Club

1991: 206,000 barrels
1992: 210,000 barrels
1993: 225,000 barrels

 ### MOUNTAIN VALLEY BREWING
122 Orange Avenue
Suffern, NY 10901   914-357-0101

Co-owners:
Lon Lanterio &
Lisa Centillo
Brewer: Jay Misson
Equipment: 7-barrel Pub system
Opened: 1992

The Mountain Valley Brewpub is in the small town of Suffern off the New York State Thruway and Highway Routes 17 and 87. The brewpub setting is amid forest, mountain streams, and rustic cabins with fireplaces. Patrons of the brewpub tend to be tourists and New York City day-trippers seeking solace in the quaint mountain setting.

A specialty of Mountain Valley's is the daily prepared "brew-b-que."

Todd Lanterio builds a fire with cherry, apple, and maple woods and adds fruit juices, water, and beer to create smoke. The meat is rubbed with herbs and spices, cooked slowly, and basted throughout the day with a special sauce.

Brewpub menu: *pubfare and locally prepared "brew-b-que"*

Pale Ale
Copper Ale
Porter
Wheat beer

1992: N/A
1993: 1,000 barrels

NEW AMSTERDAM BREWING
257 Park Avenue South, 7th Floor
New York, NY 10010   212-473-1900

Co-owners: Joe Tighe and Joe Magliocco
Brewer: John Ruhl
Equipment: Contract brewed at F. X. Matt, Utica, NY
Opened: October 1, 1982

Matthew Reich is one of the true craft brewing pioneers. He started a contract brewing operation in 1982, an innovative venture for its time, and established a new niche in the brewing industry. Some 70 second- and third- generation contract operations have copied Reich's example of having an established regional brewery produce the beer while the resources of the company are spent on developing the market via advertising and promotion.

New Amsterdam was one of 24 breweries at the first Great American Beer Festival held in 1983. It was recognized as one of the best beers at the GABF in 1983, 1984, and 1985, before medals were handed out. New Amsterdam was brewed at the F. X. Matt Brewery in upstate Utica, a fact that didn't seem to matter to consumers who fell in love with the full-flavored amber lager when it first appeared in an ocean of weaker pale pilseners.

In 1986, Reich made the decision to brew New Amsterdam in Manhattan and open a brewpub on the Lower West Side. Although the ideas had merit, the venture proved a financial disaster, and Reich lost control of the company after sinking several millions of his and investors' money into the dream. All that was left was a mountain of debts and a beer label. No one wanted the debts, but the label had value in the marketplace.

Joe Magliocci and Joe Tighe took over the ailing company in 1991. They initiated an aggressive marketing campaign that took New Amsterdam into 35 states. Tighe had a history in the brewing industry since he was 12 years old, delivering growlers of Jacob Ruppert's beers in Manhattan after Prohibition. "Babe Ruth was always down at the brewery," Tighe remembers. Ruppert was the owner of the New York Yankees, which means the Babe was either buttering up the boss or conducting his own sampling of Ruppert's wares. Either way, the Bambino was in character.

Tighe worked with several New York area breweries – Ruppert, Schaefer, Rheingold, and Ballantine – and later became vice president of an importing company selling Moosehead and Foster's. Tighe knew the value of a high-priced beer in the marketplace. He used his importing connections to line up a network of distributors to take New Amsterdam into 35 states. The effort has proved highly successful, partially because of the appeal of a New York brewed beer outside the New York area.

Tighe also came up with New Amsterdam's first holiday beer in 1992 with an artistic label. He choose Asher Durand's 1868 painting, "Dance on the Battery in the Presence of Peter Stuyvesant," for the 1992–93 Christmas label. The 1993–94 Christmas label was Tobi Kahn's "Orrah."

New Amsterdam became one of the first breweries to market Black & Tan, a style combining the ingredients of stout with ale or lager, when it released its version in 1993. New Amsterdam's beers are shipped across the country in refrigerated trucks from the Matt brewery.

New Amsterdam Ale: *a smooth, well-balanced amber ale with a dry, malty finish*
New Amsterdam Light
New Amsterdam Amber Beer: *a lager brewed with two-row malts, Cascade and Hallertauer hops; consistent medal winner at Great American Beer Festival*
New Amsterdam Black and Tan: *brewed with black and caramel malt, Kent Goldings, and Willamette hops, and ale yeast*
New Amsterdam Winter Anniversary: *a rich, malty dark lager*

1991:   N/A
1992:   N/A
1993:   N/A

OLD WORLD BREWING
2070 Victory Boulevard, Suite #4
Staten Island, NY 10314   718-370-0551

President: Sal Pennacchio
Brewer/Equipment: Contract brewed at
Point Brewing, Stevens Point, WI
Opened: February 1992

Sal Pennacchio was an award-winning homebrewer who also ran a home brew supply shop in the 1980s. Previously Pennacchio had been an analyst on Wall Street before turning a hobby into a profession. He used $250,000 of his own money to start his contract brewing operation. The name he chose, Old World Brewery, was also the name of his homebrewing supply business on Staten Island.

Pennacchio chose the Point Brewery in Stevens Point, WI, to brew his recipes for ale and porter on contract.

Harbor Ale: *a pale ale brewed with pale, caramel, Munich, and carapils malts; Chinook, Hallertau, and Cascade hops*
Harbor Ale Dark: *a porter brewed with caramel, black, and chocolate malts and Cascade hops*

1992:   1,006 barrels
1993:   1,800 barrels

ROCHESTER BREWPUB
800 Jefferson Road#
Henrietta, NY 14623   716-272-1550

President: Kevin Townsell
Brewer: Peter Black
Equipment:
Opened: April 1988

The Rochester Brewpub is part of the brewing operation started by Kevin Townsell. The Buffalo Brewpub in Williamsville was the first, and Rochester Brewpub the second. The Buffalo Brewery in nearby Lackawanna produces bottles and draft for the operation.

The Marketplace Inn is the home of the Rochester Brewpub. Henrietta's provides the dining room for the brewpub and serves breakfast, lunches, and dinners. Live Irish music is provided on Sunday nights in the brewpub.

Brewpub menu: *pubfare*

Buffalo Lager
Buffalo Pils
Buffalo Weisse
Limericks Irish Red Ale

1991: 250 barrels
1992: 360 barrels
1993: 350 barrels

⮾ ROHRBACH BREWING
315 Gregory Street
Rochester, NY 14620   716-244-5680

President: John Urlaub
Brewer: Dave Schlosser
Equipment: 7-barrel custom-design system
Opened: April 1992

Where An
Old Tradition
Becomes A New.

Founder John Urlaub was an executive with Kodak in Rochester before he left the secure world of corporate finance and marketing at the ripe age of 30 to start his own brewery. Urlaub's introduction to the world of craft brewing came when he went to the Manhattan Brewpub in 1985. He worked in Germany in 1986 and 1987 with Kodak and again saw the concept of community breweries. When Urlaub returned to the U.S. in 1987, he began homebrewing and making plans to go into business for himself. Rohrbach Brewery became the city's second brewpub when it opened in April 1992. The first, Rochester Brewing, opened in 1988. Rohrbach also serves beer from the other brewery in town, Genesee.

The Rohrbach Brewpub recalls Rochester's brewing heritage with brewiana from the city's old breweries decorating the walls. The brewpub is located in the 5,000 sq. ft. basement of the historic German House in the Swillburg neighborhood where German immigrants lived. Seating capacity in the former restaurant is 90 with another 30 in the bar.

Urlaub hired Tom Chamot to become Rohrbach's chef. Chamot's specialties include Beef and Guinness Stew and Flour City Seven Lily soup– Spanish and red onions, garlic, shallots, leeks, scallions, and chives simmered in white wine, herbs, chicken stock, and topped with melted swiss cheese. A perfect complement to the Highland Amber.

Rohrbach brews Red Wing Red, an amber ale, for the Rochester Red Wings, a AAA farm team of the Baltimore Orioles. Go Reds!

Brewpub menu: *pubfare with a few German specialties*

Sam Patch Porter
Highland Amber
Gregory Street Lager
Red Wing Red: *house beer of Rochester Red Wings baseball team*

1992:   320 barrels (opened in April)
1993:   650 barrels

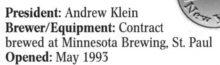

SPRING STREET BREWING
60 Spring Street
New York, NY 10012   212-226-9110

President: Andrew Klein
Brewer/Equipment: Contract brewed at Minnesota Brewing, St. Paul
Opened: May 1993

Andrew Klein was a corporate lawyer who, at 33 years old, decided his future was more in brewing and selling beer than in haunting corporate board rooms. A graduate of Harvard Law school, Klein resigned from the New York firm of Cravath, Swaine, & Moore at the 1992 Christmas office party and announced his intentions to become a brewer. Craft brewing claims another mid-life crisis casualty.

Klein choose a Belgian style "white beer" that is coming into its own on the fringes of the craft brewing world. He and his wife traveled to Europe where they visited Belgian cafes and breweries. When he chose a Belgian style to brew, Klein found a source for the exotic Belgian yeast to ferment the beer.

Klein hired consultant Dr. Joe Owades, who formulated recipes for contract beers including Samuel Adams, New Amsterdam, Olde Heurich, and Rhino Chaser.

Klein used his legal training to draw up a private stock offering that raised $500,000 to initiate his project. He also negotiated with the accounting firm, Arthur Anderson, and the marketing company of Mezzina/Brown for professional services to launch a national campaign. With the financial backing and Owades contact, Klein negotiated a contract with Minnesota Brewing in St. Paul to make his beer. Minnesota is already the brewer of Pete's Wicked Ale and Spanish Peaks contract beers.

Spring Street's sole beer, Wit, was introduced in New York in the summer of 1993. Klein introduced Wit in Washington, D.C., and plans to target urban cities where he thinks the beer will find a following. Spring Street Brewery becomes the third bottled Belgian style beer in the U.S. with Austin's Celis Brewery and Ft. Collins' New Belgium Brewery its predecessors.

Wit: *a Belgian "white" beer brewed with wheat, coriander, Curaçao orange peels, and Belgian yeast; the unusual ingredients produce a beer that has a sour, citrus taste that is refreshing and invigorating to the palate*

1993:   1,400 barrels (opened in May)

 SYRACUSE SUDS FACTORY
210-216 West Water Street
Syracuse, NY 13202   315-471-2254

President: Al Smith
Brewer: Norman Soine
Equipment:
Opened: April 17, 1993

Syracuse Suds Factory opened in 1993 in downtown Syracuse in a brick building listed in the National Register of Historic Buildings. The Erie Canal, which once transported goods from the East Coast ports to inland cities, is behind the historic building.

The brewpub is located on first two floors with the brewery located behind glass in back of the bar.

Brewpub menu: *pubfare*

Amber Ale
Pale Ale

 **WESTSIDE BREWING**
340 Amsterdam Avenue (76th Street)
New York, NY 10024   212-721-2161

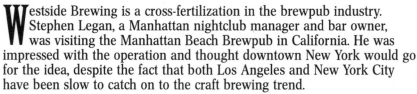

President: Stephen Legan
Brewer: William Kingsbury
Equipment: 12-barrel Bohemian system
Opened: October 1993

Westside Brewing is a cross-fertilization in the brewpub industry. Stephen Legan, a Manhattan nightclub manager and bar owner, was visiting the Manhattan Beach Brewpub in California. He was impressed with the operation and thought downtown New York would go for the idea, despite the fact that both Los Angeles and New York City have been slow to catch on to the craft brewing trend.

Legan discussed the venture with Michael Zislis, who started Manhattan Beach and two other L.A.-area brewpubs. Zislis also started his own brewing equipment concern called Bohemian Brewery Imports, which builds small breweries in Hungary. Legan was so motivated by the prospect of getting started that he hired away Manhattan Beach's brewer, William Kingsbury, to come back to the Big East to be his brewer. Boston-born and educated, Kingsbury had been looking for a chance to get back east and continue his brewing career.

Westside Brewing is a typical New York City saloon. Customers on the Upper West Side had been stopping by the corner of New Amsterdam and 76th Street since the 1930s, when Sweeney's, and later J.G. Mellon's, was in that spot. Legan kept the Irish pub facade and interior and squeezed a 12-barrel Bohemian brewery into the 2,400 sq. ft. saloon (with fermenters behind the bar and storage tanks in the basement).

New Yorkers frequent watering holes, restaurants, markets, and bakeries that have tradition and local flavor. Westside Brewing may be a modern brewpub, but it has the smell of old New York in the days of the Algonquin's Round Table, when people hung out in places called Clancy's or Fran O'Brien's. Legend has it that Ernest Hemingway drank at the mahogany bar that came from the original Sweeney's. Today, patrons belly up to the bar to soak up the saloon atmosphere and guzzle freshly brewed beer as if they're expecting Papa to stroll in.

Legan wants to start two more brewpubs in Manhattan and has locations in Greenwich Village and the Lower East Side, which he says he will open by 1995. If he does, he will be copying, the Zislis's L. A. model of metropolitan brewpub chains.

Kingsbury probably has one of the smallest working areas of any modern brewer–approximately 60 square feet against the back wall. Connecting pipes, the control panel, faucets, and gauges make it appear like a Rube Goldberg nightmare.

Brewpub menu: *pubfare*

Blonde Light Lager
Real Ale
Nut Brown: *a medium-bodied brown ale with reddish brown color and malty aftertaste*
Pale Ale: *mildly bitter ale with a short aftertaste; brewed with Cascade and Clusters hops*
Raspberry Ale: *the holiday beer with the essence of raspberries in the aroma and a pleasant, sweet aftertaste*

1993: N/A (opened in October)

 **WOODSTOCK BREWING**
  20 St. James Street
  Kingston, NY 12401   914-331-2810

President/brewer: Nat Collins
Equipment: 20-barrel DME system
Opened: February 1992

The Woodstock Brewery is blessed by more than its riverfront location in the scenic Hudson Valley, home to some 22 breweries during the 19th century. The brewery's name and its founder harken back to the 1970s, when free spirited youth frolicked in nearby pastures one summer listening to rock and roll, smoking dope, drinking who knows what, making love on blankets, and blazing a lasting imprint on modern culture. That Woodstock spirit is still alive today in the corners of people's memories – and in the craft brewery that bears its name.

Woodstock's founder, Nat Collins, was born in Mexico and developed a taste for travel at an early age. He ended up in the Hudson Valley during the 1970s. Collins lived in the Rainbow Farm commune in Phoenicia and worked as a carpenter, farmer, beekeeper, and homebrewer. After he left the commune, he remained in the Hudson Valley because of its easy-going life-style, natural beauty, and historical legacy.

Collins worked in a health food store, gourmet food store, and restaurant before he started his own construction company, which he managed until 1990. But the urge to travel and seek new horizons was still a part of his psyche. The idea of having his own brewery held a strong appeal to him, and he took a year off to tour microbreweries and take a course at the U.S. Brewers Academy in Chicago.

When he returned to the Hudson Valley, he came across a foundry built in 1830. Kingston once had five breweries; the last, Barmann's, closed in 1942. The scenic Hudson Valley is in the heart of America's colonial brewing tradition. The Woodstock Brewery is near Kingston's Stockade area originally settled by the Dutch in the 17th century. During the Revolutionary War, the area was burned by the British Army.

Colllins sold his first Hudson Lager in February 1992 to a local restaurant. His business is focused on local restaurants and taverns with approximately 100 Hudson Valley accounts. He plans to add a bottling line and produce seasonal beers named for the area's traditions and legends. One will become Ichabod Crane Ale.

Hudson Lager: *an amber-colored lager brewed with Hallertau and Tettnang hops*
Roundout Stout
St. James Ale

1992:   1,000 barrels
1993:   1,200 barrels

ZIP CITY BREWING
3 West 18th Street
New York, NY 10011   212-366-6333

President: Kirby Shyer
Brewer: Jack Streich
Equipment: 12-barrel Salm system from Austria
Opened: November 1991

Kirby Shyer was working for the family optometry business but itching for a chance to prove himself in his own business. He read about New Amsterdam contract brewer Matthew Reich in the 1980s, when Reich was making news as New York's first brewer. Shyer traveled out West and visited brewpubs in Utah and Washington. He was determined to bring the idea to life in Manhattan despite the reputation New York City had as a tough beer market. (Reich's New Amsterdam went bankrupt in 1990.)

Shyer raised about $700,000 with money from family and investors in New York, Austria and Hong Kong. He found a location for his Manhattan brewpub in the Flatiron area, that was once the center for the ladies garment trade. The building he found was built in 1895 as the headquarters of the National Temperance Society at the turn of the century. The society published temperance literature and claimed that in 1900, New York was the home of 288 breweries!

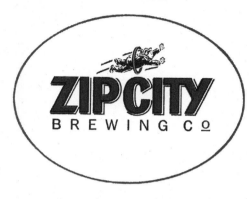

Shyer eventually raised $1.25 million to open Zip City with a name derived from a Sinclair Lewis novel, *Babbitt*. Shyer says his mother suggested it when they were trying to come up with a name that evoked Manhattan's "Gotham city" reputation.

Zip City is in a narrow, long, 6,600 sq. ft. building with a mezzanine for private parties. The brew kettle is squeezed into the narrow bar in the center of the brewpub. Small tables are recessed into the walls in the front of the brewpub. Two-liter glass growlers were instituted in 1993 for take-home trade.

When Zip City's brewing equipment was brought into the building, they had to use a freight elevator and knock out the walls to get them downstairs. The computer-controlled brewing system upstairs is heated with a gas-fired basement boiler. Additional fermentation and storage tanks were added in 1993 to allow three different beers on draft at all times. Zip City produces only unfiltered and unpasteurized lagers which are stored for at least a month in the basement. Fool's Gold, a smoked pilsener was brewed for Zip City in 1994 by Mountain Valley Brewpub in Suffern. When Shyer married Jennifer Brown on May 28, a Bride's Bock Maibock was brewed for the reception held at Zip City.

Beer dinners (some with cigars), tastings, and special events are a part of Zip City's ambitious plan to make it in New York. The menu is important for any New York restaurant, and Chef Peter Spinelli presents many features like littleneck clams steamed with pilsener and apple cider, yellow-fin tuna chili, pulled pork, and pizza with beer-dough crust.

Brewpub menu: *lunches and dinners*

Helles: *pale, light bodied lager*
Maerzen: *reddish amber lager*
Eisbock: *holiday beer*

Pilsener
Vienna
Dunkel
Rauchbier

1991: **70 barrels** (opened in November)
1992: **1,127 barrels**
1993: **1,700 barrels**

ALLEGHENY BREWING COMPANY/ PENNSYLVANIA BREWING
Troy Hill Road & Vinial Street
Pittsburgh, PA 15212   412-237-9402

President: Tom Pastorius
Brewer: Alexander Deml
Equipment: 30 hectoliter brewhouse designed by Jacob Carl Goeppingen in Germany
Opened: April 1991

Tom Pastorius and his wife, Mary Beth, lived in Germany for a decade and observed that breweries made an impact on local life, culture, and cuisine. When the North American craft brewing revolution began, the Pastoriuses wanted to re-create that German tradition in their home in Pittsburgh. Originally Tom contracted to have a beer brewed for him, Pennsylvania Pilsener, at the Pittsburgh Brewing Company. The agreement, however, prevented him from selling it in Pittsburgh even though it was brewed there in his home town.

That kind of restriction was too much of a burden for Pastorius, who lives the craft brewing experience as a personal crusade. He was determined to open a brewery in Pittsburgh because of its rich brewing heritage. He purchased the former century-old Eberhard & Ober Brewery, which used to brew Dutch Club and E & O Pilsner from 1848–1952.

He and Mary Beth spent three years and $4 million restoring the structure to build their Allegheny brewpub which opened in September 1989. A Ratskeller party room and lagering cellar, which reportedly cost another $1.5 million, opened in June 1992. The Allegheny brewpub is a classic German beer hall with solid maple tables in the beer hall, a spacious Ratskellar, a biergarten with hanging geraniums in the summer, and a German oompah band on festival occasions. The brewpub is listed in the National Register of Historical Places and started a revival of the old Deutsch North Side.

Allegheny is one of the few authentic German beer halls in the U.S.– somewhat of a rarity in the American craft brewing experience. Only Stoudt Brewery in Adamstown, Oldenberg in Ft. Mitchell, Kentucky, and Sudwerk in Davis, California, have succeeded at this German theme brewpub.

Brewer Alexander Deml is a graduate of the Weihenstephan Technical Brewing Institute in Munich. He supervised the installation of Allegheny's German-made brewery. Allegheny brews a wide variety of traditional German beer styles: pilsener, light lager, dark lager, Kaiser pils, Oktoberfest, Celebrator Bock, alt, maerzen, weizen, and weizen bock.

Brewpub menu: *Germany specialties from Rostbraten Und Kummel and Kaiserburger Brotzeis (sandwiches), suppen, salat, and Wurstplatte, Hecht Filet, Paprika Huehnchen, Schweinebraten, Wiener Schnitzel*

Penn Light Lager: *a helles beer; gold medal winner in Munchner helles category at 1993 Great American Beer Festival*
Kaiser Pils: *classic German pilsener, light, clear, mildly dry and hoppy*
Penn Pilsner: *premium lager*
Penn Dark: *dark Munich lager*
Alt
Bock
Maerzen
Wieizen
Weizen Bock
Oktoberfest
Celebrator Bock

1991:	6,000 barrels
1992:	7,000 barrels
1993:	7,500 barrels

 ARROWHEAD BREWING
1667 Orchard Drive
Chambersburg, PA 17201   717-264-0101

President:
Francis Mead
Brewers: Francis Mead
& Vince Hagen
Equipment: 25-barrel Pub Brewing system
Opened: November 1991

Francis Mead was in the pharmaceutical business in Philadelphia with Smith, Kleine, and French when he developed an itch to strike out on his own. With degrees in biology and pharmacology research, a brewing career was not exactly a radical departure, since most of Fran's work had been in laboratory doing drug research and development.

Mead (what a charming name for a brewer!) began brewing at home in 1986. When he began researching the brewing option, he went to Portland, Maine to work as an apprentice at the Geary brewery with Alan Pugsley, who had designed many East Coast breweries.

When Mead and his wife, Cynthia, made the decision to change careers and move out of the big city, they looked around for a suitable location. They settled on Chambersburg, a modest community a 30-minute drive from historic Gettysburg. This rural area is known for raising dairy cattle, growing apples and corn and just happened to be nearly equidistant from Philadelphia, Pittsburgh, Washington, and Baltimore where the combined population is over 10 million. Many of those folks are developing a powerful taste for craft beers.

The Arrowhead Brewery is located in a new industrial park on Interstate 81 parallel to Highway 11, the Molly Pitcher Highway. According to lore, Pitcher provided water to Union troops during the Civil War.

Arrowhead's annual brewing capacity is 6,000 barrels. Arrowhead's sole beer, a pale ale, is sold in bottles and draft.

Arrowhead Pale Ale: *traditional English pale ale brewed with British pale malt, crystal, chocolate and wheat; Cascade and Northern Brewer hops used for bittering*

1991: 300 barrels (opened in November)
1992: 1,600 barrels
1993: 2,400 barrels

DOCK STREET BREWING COMPANY
2 Logan Square, 18th & Cherry Streets
Philadelphia, PA 19103   215-496-0413

President: Jeffrey Ware
Brewer: Nicholas Funnell
Equipment: 8-barrel JV Northwest system
Opened: October 1990

Jeffrey Ware leveraged his success with his Dock Street contract beer to raise $2.6 million to build a downtown Philadelphia brewpub. He opened his classic brewpub in 1990 with a formula combining contemporary American atmosphere with British pub traditions in food and beer.

The 7,500 sq. ft. brewpub features cherry woods, accented by gleaming copper brew kettles, columns, terra cotta tiles and granite bartops in the dining room. An adjoining billiard room with antique pool tables and

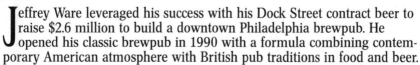

dart boards accommodates the sporting customer seeking competitive diversions. Behind the bar is an impressive mural painted by local artist Tom Judd.

Brewer Nick Funnell is from London and holds a chemistry degree from the University of Leeds. He was head brewer at Clifton Inns in London, where he supervised brewing at five brewpubs. His specialties are cask-conditioned "real ales," a rarity in the U.S., but standard brewing fare in Great Britain. Cask-conditioned ale undergoes secondary fermentation in casks and is drawn, usually by hand pumps, without filtering. Funnell brews more than a dozen traditional English and German beers year round.

Manager Jim Tourtillotte worked with Hyatt Regency, Houlihans, and Al E. Gators in Haverford before joining the Dock Street operation in 1992.

Ware plans on using the model of Philadelphia's Dock Street Brewpub to springboard into other Big East cities with Washington, D.C., his first target. Washington's Dock Street will be located at 13th street off Pennsylvania in the downtown "brewery corridor" and is scheduled to open in 1994.

Brewpub menu: *continental specialties like rabbit cassoulet, Muscovy duck chili; traditional British pub fare, chicken pot pie, shepherd's pie, and Cornish pastries*

Bohemian pils
Helles
Weiss
Porter
India Pale Ale
Cream Ale: *silver medal winner in cream ale category at 1992 Great American Beer Festival*
Extra Special bitter

1991:   1,500 barrels
1992:   1,500 barrels
1993:   1,500 barrels

DOCK STREET BREWING
225 City Line Avenue, Suite #100
Bala Cynwyd, PA 19004   215-668-1480

President: Jeffrey Ware
Brewers/Equipment: William Moeller & Mortimer Brenner;
contract brewed at F. X. Matt, NY
Opened: September 1986

hiladelphia has a rich brewing heritage that dates from the 1680s when the town was first colonized by the Dutch and Germans. Philadelphia was at one time home to more than 100 breweries, many of which exported beer to other colonies and states after the Revolutionary War. Philadelphia's advantage was its utility as one of the major East Coast ports. The City of Brotherly Love is located at the junction of the Susquehana and the Delaware rivers, which empty into Atlantic Ocean. In colonial days, Philadelphia was a busy seaport handling goods from all the colonies as well as the nations of the Old World.

Jeffrey Ware, a native Philadelphian and chef, wanted to give the city another chance to appreciate local beer. He started Dock Street Brewing in 1986 and had his beer made in upstate New York at the Matt Brewery. Ware named his brewery Dock Street after a well-known thoroughfare in old Philadelphia where several pubs and taverns thrived in the 18th and 19th centuries.

Ware has a background working in city restaurants as pastry chef at Wildflowers and chef at the Fish Market before he started Dock Street with an initial investment of only $20,000. He eventually raised more than $100,000 and used his success with the contract beer to start a brewpub by the same name. Ware raised an additional $1 million with limited partners, bank loans, and redevelopment financing to open his brewpub in Philadelphia's financial district.

Dock Street Amber Beer: *an American ale brewed with two-row pale and caramel malts, dry hopped with Cascade hops; gold medal from Mondie Selection in Brussels; silver medal for cream ale at 1992 Great American Beer Festival*
Dock Street Bohemian Pilsner: *a golden-colored traditional pilsener, mellow, smooth taste; brewed with Zatec and Hallertau hops*

1991:   10,000 barrels
1992:   12,000 barrels
1993:   14,000 barrels

JONES BREWING
254 Second Street
Smithton, PA 15479   412-872-6626

President: Gabriel "Gabby" Podlucky
Brewer: Greg King
Equipment: 150-barrel American system built in 1907
Opened: 1907

William "Stoney" Jones was a Welsh immigrant who came to America and bought the Eureka Brewing Company, founded in 1881, in Smithton, south of Pittsburgh. Jones Brewing is today one a of handful of small, regional breweries that survived first Prohibition, later mergers, consolidations, and closures of hundreds of breweries.

The original beer produced by Eureka was called Eureka Crown Gold. But foreign-speaking immigrants in Pennsylvania had a hard time pronouncing it, so the name was changed to "Stoney" after the owner's nickname. "Stoney" Jones was the grandfather of actress Shirley Jones.

In July 1988, Gabriel and Sandy Podlucky purchased the Jones Brewery and invested in new capital equipment. They began an aggressive marketing campaign throughout the region and abroad. The first shipment of Stoney's to Korea was made in 1993.

Smithton is 30 miles south of Pittsburgh near the intersection of Exit 8 on the Pennsylvania Turnpike and Interstate 70. Jones also brews on contract for the Allegheny Brewing (Penn Pilsener) in Pittsburgh, the Mill Bakery, Eatery, and Brewery chain in Florida, Georgia, and Alabama, and several private label draft beers. Stoney's Light became Hog Brew sold in Washington, D.C., after the Redskins won the Super Bowl in 1991.

Stoney has become something of a darling in the entertainment industry, with several guest appearances in movies and TV. The beer appeared in a remake of the cult classic, *Night of the Living Dead*, which was shot near Pittsburgh, and in *Bob Roberts*, and *The Cemetery Club*. During the 1994 TV season, Stoney's will be featured on CBS's popular show, *Northern Exposure*.

Jones was one of the first to brew "dry" beer when it came out with Esquire Extra Dry in 1989. Jones's brewer, Greg King, is the great-grandson of founder "Stoney Jones."

Stoney's Beer: *silver medal winner in American lager category at 1991 Great American Beer Festival*
Stoney's Light: *silver medal in American light lager category at 1991 GABF*
Esquire Extra Dry: *bronze medal winner at 1991 GABF and silver medal winner in American dry lager category at 1993 GABF*
Esquire: *the Jones premium beer*
Fort Pitt
Old Shay Cream Ale

1991: 55,852 barrels
1992: 75,000 barrels
1993: 89,000 barrels

 ## LATROBE BREWING
119 Jefferson Street
Latrobe, PA 15650   412-537-5545

Owners: Labatts, USA
Brewmaster: Mike Fitzpatrick
Equipment: 600 barrel brewhouse
Opened: 1893

Latrobe Brewery opened in 1893 in a railroad and mining town 45 miles east of Pittsburgh to serve the western Pennsylvania coal miners. The brewery closed six years later when the Pittsburgh breweries were all combining under the Pittsburgh Brewing Company.

In 1932, with the momentum mounting for Repeal of Prohibition, five local brothers from Latrobe–Frank, Joseph, Robert, Ralph, and Anthony Trio–bought the brewery from its owners. The brewery produced the same beers as those produced before Prohibition but believed they needed a new product to distinguish the new era in brewing.

In 1939, the Trio family came up with a new brand name, Rolling Rock, a tribute to the western Pennsylvania mountain terrain and the mountain spring water used to brew the beer. Rolling Rock is most often packaged in green, long-neck bottles with an applied ceramic or "painted" label. Although attractive and popular, the painted label is expensive and labor intensive; it costs almost 50 cents more per six-pack to produce than the conventional paper label bottle.

Fifty years later, Rolling Rock is still sold in the original bottles painted green with the legend of "33" on the back. Local legends and myths have surrounding the meaning of the "33." One popular explanation was that it referred to the year 1933 when

Prohibition was repealed; another that it was the number of words on the back of the bottle.

Latrobe was experiencing labor problems in the early 1980s and faced a possible shutdown as production declined. In 1987, the brewery was bought by the Labatt's USA, of Darien, Connecticut, a subsidiary of the giant Canadian brewery. Labatts raised the price of Rolling Rock to that of the popular price brands and conducted an aggressive marketing and advertising campaign with radio, television, and billboard ads.

The effort succeeded and even went beyond what marketing experts projected. Latrobe has shown a 13% growth in sales each year since the takeover, growing from a low of 420,000 barrels in 1985 to more than 1 million barrels in 1993. Although Rolling Rock is sold in select markets around the country, 70% of sales are still in the Big East home region of Latrobe. In 1993, Latrobe introduced the latest product, Rolling Rock Bock.

Rolling Rock: *a premium lager*
Rolling Rock Bock

1991:   803,000 barrels
1992:   840,000 barrels
1993:   1,046,000 barrels

THE LION, INC.
700 North Pennsylvania Ave
Wilkes-Barre, PA 18703   717-823-8801

Owner: Quincy Partners, Inc.
Brewers: Phil Leinhart, Guy Hagner, Leo Orlandini
Equipment: 390-barrel brewhouse manufactured in Hoboken, NJ, in 1954
Opened: 1857

Wilkes-Barre's Lion Brewery has been known by many names in its more than a century of brewing in the Wyoming Valley. It originally was the Luzerne County Brewery and became the Lion Brewery in 1910. During Prohibition, the Lion Brewery made "buck-o" cereal beverage. After Repeal, the brewery was purchased by the Smulowitz and Swarz brothers who renamed it the Lion. From 1943 to 1977, the name was changed to the Gibbons Brewery.

When many of Pennsylvania's breweries were closing after Repeal, the Lion/Gibbons Breweries bought the old labels and made the beer. One of the beers they made was the Stegmaier, which at one time was one of Pennsylvania's largest breweries. Its founder, Charles Stegmaier, reportedly delivered beer in a goat cart around Wilkes-Barre when all breweries were local.

During the Golden Age of Brewing in the late 19th century and early 20th century before the Great War, Stegmaier won medals at international beer expositions. Stegmaier won the Grand Premio Vittorio Emmanuel in Rome in 1911, the Exposition International Medal at Antwerp in 1911, the Austrian Gold Cross of Excellence in 1913, and the Franz Josef Medal in Vienna in 1913. It also won the American-Canadian Grand Award in Brussels in 1950 and again in 1956.

The Lion is just off Interstate 81 in a dingy Wilkes-Barre industrial yard alongside the railroad tracks. The Lion looks like an old brewery graveyard. Although the Lion's annual brewing capacity is 250,000 barrels, only a small percentage of this is beer.

In more recent times, Lion has survived by becoming a contract brewer and bottler of soft drinks, coolers, and malta, a non-alcoholic beverage made from malt. The Stoudt Brewery in Adamstown, Blue Hen in Delaware, and the Manhattan Brewery contract brewed at the Lion.

In 1993 nearly 75% of the product made at The Lion was malta for the New York and New Jersey markets.

McSorley's Ale House, one of New York's classic pubs in Greenwich Village, had its beer made at the Lion at one time. The Lion also brewed Nude Beer which experienced notoriety in the late 1980's.

Stegmaier 1857: *a premium all-malt lager named for the date the brewery opened*

1991: N/A
1992: 58,327 barrels
1993: 50,000 barrels

 PITTSBURGH BREWING
3340 Liberty Avenue
Pittsburgh, PA 15201   412-682-7400

President: Jack Isherwood
Brewer: Mike Carota
Equipment: Two 600-barrel Enerfab systems
Opened: 1861

Pittsburgh Brewing is one of the old-line industrial breweries that has survived the turmoil and disruptions that American breweries suffered in the last 100 years. The brewery started in 1861 when Edward Frauenheim opened a brewery to brew Iron City Beer, one of the first lagers brewed in America.

In 1873, Frauenheim formed a partnership with Leopold Vilsack, and the two opened the Frauenheim and Vilsack Brewery at 34th Street and Liberty Avenue in downtown Pittsburgh. They changed the name to the Iron City Brewery to capitalize on the identity with the steel industry. Andrew Carnegie, J. P. Mellon, and the robber barons owned Pittsburgh and everything was tied into iron and steel.

In 1899, 21 Pittsburgh breweries merged with Iron City Brewing to form Pittsburgh Brewing. It became the state's largest brewery and the third largest in the U.S. Almost a century later, the brewery is still at the site on Liberty Avenue where Frauenheim and Vilsack started their Iron City Brewery in 1873.

During Prohibition, Pittsburgh Brewing made ice cream, soft drinks, and near beer to survive. Pittsburgh was one of some three hundred breweries to survive Repeal and the Depression shakeout by making frequent innovations. Pittsburgh was the first brewery to use the snap-top can developed by Alcoa, another Pittsburgh corporate giant. Pittsburgh was the first to use twists-off resealable caps and to put local sports teams on beer cans. Hometown favorites, the Penguins, Pirates, Steelers, and the University of Pittsburgh Panthers have all graced the aluminum containers which today are treasured by brewiana collectors.

Pittsburgh was one of the first to come up with light beer when it introduced I.C. Light in 1977. In more recent times, Pittsburgh was purchased in 1985 by the giant Swan Brewing, Ltd., of Australia. After a disastrous financial setback due to accumulated debt, Swan sold the brewery back to a Pittsburgh entrepreneur, Michael Carlow, in 1992.

Once considered a blue-collar beer in a beer-and-a-bump town, Pittsburgh Brewing has benefited from the craft brewing movement by becoming one of the principal regional breweries for upscale contract beers. In vats that once aged only Iron City and its light derivatives came "The Best Beer in America," the high-priced Samuel Adams Boston Lager, and other premium contract beers. When Samuel Adams annual production grew into the hundred thousand of barrels per year category, owner Jim Koch had to find other regional breweries to supplement his output at Pittsburgh.

Pittsburgh has tried a succession of beers to ignite local interest after watching the success of East Coast craft brewers. I.C. Golden Lager and J. J. Wainwright's Select Lager Beer were two brands added to the Iron City line. The brewery has also been a consistent exporter of beer to Russia and the former nations of the Soviet Union.

Iron City Beer
I.C. Light
I.C. Golden Lager
J. J. Wainwright's
American Light lager
American Light

1991: 1,000,000 barrels
1992: 1,000,000 barrels
1993: 990,000 barrels

SAMUEL ADAMS BREW HOUSE
1516 Sansom Street
Philadelphia, PA 19102   215-563-2326

President: Dave Mink
Brewer: Jim Pericles
Equipment: 7-barrel system
Opened: November 1989

Dave Mink ran a family restaurant, the Sansom Street Oyster House, in downtown Philadelphia when he heard Jim Koch of Boston Beer Company deliver a lecture at the Wharton School on craft brewing. He talked to Koch after the lecture and asked if he would be interested in a brewpub venture in Philadelphia. The two entered into an agreement with Mink licensing the name Sam Adams and the two sharing costs and revenues.

The Samuel Adams Brew House is the upstairs of the Oyster House, a popular seafood restaurant that has been in business since 1976. Oysters are a traditional Philadelphia dish that goes back to colonial times when they were harvested on the banks of the Delaware River. Mink has oysters shipped in weekly from Washington, Maine, Virginia, and New Jersey. One of the specialties is a platter of eight oysters from the northeast, mid-Atlantic, and northwest waters. A waiter or waitress guides patrons through the assortment and discusses the origins of each and their subtle tastes and textures. There is as much difference in the varieties of oysters as there are in craft beers.

Jim Pericles, a local homebrewer, was hired as Samuel Adams's first brewer in the summer of 1989. He traveled to Boston to work with the brewers at Boston Beer and plans to transfer to Boston in 1994. The Samuel Adams Brew House is a rare commodity – a malt extract system. Although once common in Canada, extract breweries have not done well in the U.S. Hops and yeast are shipped from Boston, and the brewers consult on recipes and brewing procedures.

When it opened in November 1989, Samuel Adams became Philadelphia's first new brewery since the Repeal of Prohibition. The atmosphere at Sam Adams is similar to what one might find at a local pub on a narrow London side street. The pub's entrance is reached by climbing the stairs to the second floor. Patrons are greeted by the friendly "publican" behind the bar who acts as host, bartender, and social director. The pubs has a homey, old-time character with dark carpeting, small tables, and photos of Philadelphia sports heroes on the walls. Philadelphia is a serious sports town with rabid fans supporting college basketball (Temple,

Villanova, Penn, and Drexel) and professional teams (Phillies, Eagles, Sixers, and Flyers).

The original pub was only 2,000 sq. ft., but that was increased to 3,500 for more tables. The brewery is along one wall next to the bar. Sam Adams Brew House can accommodate only about 70 people with another 15 at the bar; cozy but not cramped. The brew kettle is heated with 3 electric coils that bring the mash to a slow boil. The brew kettle, fermenters, and a cold box holding the storage tanks are in a line along the wall.

The recession has hit Philadelphia restaurants hard, and the Samuel Adams Brew House has instituted promotions to let customers know they are still around. Live music on the weekend, a sports call-in radio show, and homebrew competitions are a few of the programs to attract customers.

Brewpub menu: *burgers, salads, pubfare*

Ben Franklin's Golden Ale: *a light golden ale brewed with Northern Brewer and Hallertau hops; light, crisp taste with short finish*
Poor Richard's Amber Ale: *light amber color, slight malty taste*
George Washington's Porter: *a dark ruby color, brewed with Northern Brewer, Kent Goldings, and Hallertau hops and honey; a medium-bodied porter with a sweet, slight licorice aftertaste*
Peppered Golden Ale: *a few grams of jalopena peppers are chopped and added in storage vessels of a batch of Golden Ale; the result is a mild, pepper tasting ale that leaves a lingering tickle on the throat*

1991: 700 barrels
1992: 700 barrels
1993: 700 barrels

 STOUDT BREWERY
Route 272
Adamstown, PA 19501   215-484-4387

President: Carol Stoudt
Brewer: Bill Moore
Equipment: 15 barrel JV Northwest system
Opened: June 1987

South-central Pennsylvania is a tourist mecca for harried New Yorkers and New Jerseyans looking to exchange urban congestion for the pastoral life of rural of Lancaster County. The area was made famous by the Harrison Ford and Kelley McGillis movie *Witness* about the clash between rural Amish values and grisly urban crime. The classic barn-raising episode and the towheaded children working hard in farm and field recall a time in America when agriculture was the basis of the country's economy and the "simple" rural life was an ideal we seem to have lost.

Carol and Ed Stoudt owned a successful German-style family restaurant, the Black Angus, in Adamstown and had a loyal following of patrons who came to have dinner, shop for antiques in their gift shop, and have a beer in the outdoor beer garden. When the Stoudts first heard about brewpubs starting on the West Coast in the mid 1980s, they went to California for a look and fell in love with the idea. They knew how they could make the concept work back home in Adamstown.

The Stoudts hired Karl Strauss, formerly Master Brewer at Pabst, to help them build the brewery and formulate the beers. But problems arose when they couldn't get a license because state regulations forbade someone having a liquor license from also having a brewing license. The simple solution was to put the brewery in Carol's name; she then sells the beer back to Black Angus owned by Ed. The Stoudt Brewery was the first craft brewery in Pennsylvania, a state that once had hundreds of regional breweries. Their home country, Lancaster County, had 36 breweries at one time.

Carol is one of the few women brewers in the craft brewing industry. She has established her brewery as one of the leaders in the country. Stoudt's is one of the top medal winners at the Great American Festival capturing 15 medals since 1990–93. In 1992, they won four medals, including gold for their Oktoberfest and Export, tying another craft brewery, the North Coast Brewery in Ft. Bragg, CA, in the medal count. In 1993, Stoudt won three medals at the GABF.

The Stoudts jumped onto the beer festival wagon in 1992 when they held their first mid-Atlantic festival in June. The festival attracted 17 mid-Atlantic and northeast breweries (no contract brewers were allowed) and sold out their allotted 1,500 tickets in a few days. They expanded to a two-day festival in 1993 and had two sessions on Saturday.

The Stoudt Brewery is located on Route 272 just off exit 21 on the Pennsylvania Turnpike. One of Stoudt's many features is the casual hominess where visitors sip fresh beers, eat German foods, enjoy the Pennsylvania mountains, and shop for antiques. It's a great way to spend a lazy weekend.

Brewpub menu: *German and American fare with outdoor dining in bier garden*

Stoudt's Pilsener: *moderately hopped German-style pilsener; gold medal winner at 1993 Great American Beer Festival*
Stoudt's Export Gold: *gold medal winner at 1992 GABF; brewed with five roasted malts, German Hallertau and Tettnanger hops*
Stoudt's Fest: *light amber, malty, well hopped lager, gold medal winner in Oktoberfest category at 1992 GABF*
Stoudt's Bock: *silver medal winner at 1992 and 1993 GABF*
Stoudt's Ale: *reddish amber, well hopped English-style bitters*
Stoudt's Double Bock: *silver medal winner at 1992 GABF; dark color and sweet, malty aftertaste*

1991:   1,200 barrels
1992:   1,800 barrels
1993:   4,200 barrels

 STRAUB BREWERY
303 Sorg Street
St. Mary's, PA 15857   814-834-2875

Co-Presidents: Thomas Straub & Daniel Straub
Brewer: Thomas Straub
Equipment: 150-barrel system built in 1901 and acquired from the St. Mary's Brewery
Opened: 1876

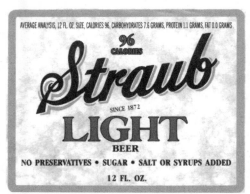

The Straub family brewery founder Peter Straub was born in 1840 in Felldorff, Wurtemburg, Germany and worked as a cooper in a local brewery. He immigrated to the U.S. in 1869 and lived in Allegheny City, Pennsylvania, north of Pittsburgh, where he worked for the Eberhardt and Ober Brewery. He moved to St. Mary's in the Allegheny Mountains in 1872 to work as brewmaster for the Volk's Brewery and Saloon, which he bought in 1876 and moved to its present site.

The Straub Brewery was one of only 120 Pennsylvania breweries that survived Prohibition. In 1947, when the brewery was incorporated, six Straub family members from two generations were named as corporate officers.

Founder Peter Straub's great-grandsons, Thomas J. and Daniel A. Straub, are sharing responsibilities to keep the brewery in the family. Tradition is still a part of the family brewery; visitors to the brewery can pour as much beer as they like from the Eternal Tap that is always open to workers and visitors. On opening day of deer season, brewery workers are given a paid holiday to go hunting.

Straub uses corn flakes in addition to malted barley to produce its beers. Straub's beers are sold throughout Pennsylvania and Eastern Ohio. Every tavern in Elk County, where St. Mary's is located, carries Straub on tap. Patrons who want a Straub ask for a "greenie," the color of the Straub bottle.

Straub Beer
Straub Light

1991: 26,000 barrels
1992 26,300 barrels
1993: N/A

YUENGLING BREWING
5th & Mahantongo Streets
Pottsville, PA 17901   717-622-4141

President: Richard Yuengling
Brewer: N. Ray Norbert
Equipment: 450-barrel brewhouse
Opened: 1829

The Yuengling Brewery has a long and colorful history–it is the oldest brewery in America, surviving through more than 160 years of political turmoil, economic difficulties, and national expansion. When David Yuengling opened the Eagle Brewery on Centre Street in Pottsville in 1829, Andrew Jackson was President, and we were a nation of only 30 states, and the Louisiana Purchase territory was only beginning to be explored.

When the Eagle Brewery burned in 1831, Yuengling moved it to the side of a mountain in Pottsville. Yuengling chose this location so he could store (or lager) his beer in the mountain's caves to produce a traditional German beer even though modern-day lager style had yet to be brewed in Europe. The German miners who mined coal in the Pennsylvania mountains preferred beer that had been aged at cold temperatures for several months.

What started out as a good idea for a small brewery in Pennsylvania coal country brought a set of problems David Yuengling could not have predicted in the 1830s. When he was alive, his beer was delivered by horse-drawn wagons to taverns in downtown Pottsville. A century later, Yuengling beer is delivered by the 18-wheel monsters navigating the nation's interstate highways and turnpikes. Today, Yuengling's beers are sold in places far from Center County, which means large refrigerated trucks must struggle up Pottsville's steep hills and down narrow streets to pick up beer brewed in the same hillside brewery and stored in the same caves as they were more than 160 years ago.

The Yuengling Brewery looks like a century-old brewery should look–dignified, proud, imposing, and a little worn around the edges. From the top of Mahantongo Street, the brewery looks over the valley where it has played a major role in the local economy and culture since the first German settlers arrived in the early 19th century. Visitors taking the daily tours walk down hallways, through the brewing plant, and into caves where generations of brewery workers toiled more than a century ago.

Richard Yuengling, great-great grandson of David Yuengling, began working in the brewery at the age of 15, when he moved kegs and worked on the loading dock. He left the family business for a few years and worked with one of the local beer distributors. He took over the family business from his father and became president in 1985, the fifth generation to lead the family brewery. But future family plans for brewery management are indefinite; Richard has four daughters in their late teens and early 20s.

Dick Yuengling was fortunate to take over at a time when craft breweries were reacquainting the nation with its beer heritage. The Yuengling Brewery had suffered like all regional breweries after the Repeal of Prohibition and the wave of mergers and consolidations. Since the end of World War II, Americans were drinking less beer and preferring the large national brands advertised on television. The time for regional breweries like Yuengling's had come and gone–until the early 1980s when craft breweries began capturing the attention and support of consumers.

In 1991, Dick Yuengling made a decision to join the revolution. He added three new styles–a light, amber lager, and Black and Tan, to attract the new generation of craft beer drinkers. The effort succeeded handsomely and production rose from 120,000 barrels in 1991 to more than 200,000 in 1992, and 246,000 in 1993. At one time, Yuengling was the only brewer of porter left in the country–today it is the largest brewery of porter in the U.S.

A new addition to the brewery is a museum and gift shop for the 20,000 visitors who come to Pottsville every year. On display are old Yuengling brewiana from the brewery's 165 years. Photos of the old brewery, workers toiling in the caves, and the old bottles and posters make the museum one of the most authentic displays of American brewing history in the country.

Yuengling has seen incredible revival of interest in its beers in the 1990s. Despite the expansion started in 1992, the brewery has experienced growing pains. Although the brewery is making almost twice as much beer as it was in 1990, it has had to cut back on shipments to large markets which had "rediscovered" Yuengling–New York, Maryland, Virginia, the District of Columbia, and New England. Yuengling's first priority is to meet the demand in the home markets of Pennsylvania, New Jersey, and Delaware.

Throughout its long history, Yuengling's label has remained the same–an American eagle with its wings spread with one claw clutching a wooden barrel. Yuengling's local reputation is long lasting and affectionate–it is known as "vitamin Y."

Yuengling Premium: *largest volume brand, a mild medium-bodied lager*
Yuengling Lager: *a light lager*
Yuengling Light
Lord Chesterfield Ale: *a light amber, medium bodied ale*
Porter: *an old-time favorite for beer lovers before the craft brewing revolution revived styles like porter; a lighter bodied porter than other craft porters, but a pleasant and smooth-tasting brew*
Black & Tan: *derived from the 18th-century English tradition of mixing porter and ale to give a dark colored, but mild-tasting ale. Yuengling revived this tradition with its own recipe (60% porter and 40% premium) and has had great success in marketing the product*

1991:   160,000 barrels
1992:   210,810 barrels
1993:   240,000 barrels

BARDO RODEO
2000 Wilson Blvd.
Arlington, VA 22201   703-527-1852

President: Bill Stewart
Brewer: Steve Allen
Equipment: 20-barrel Century system
Opened: November 1993

BARDO RODEO

Bardo Rodeo is a Twin Peaks kind of place: comfortable with its grunge look and dogged following of late night crowds seeking a real experience. With Washington being an uptight city where impressing your peers is a requisite for professional advancement, Bardo is a place where one can kick back, be outrageous, and not be responsible for "socially correct" behavior. Don't expect ferns or Barry Manilow crooning from the jukebox; Bardo looks more like a rundown garage (which in truth it is) or a fraternity basement (which might object to the comparison).

The force behind Bardo is Bill Stewart, an MIT-educated designer whose passion for bizarre "car art" seems to be unfulfilled. Stewart was an artist in Boston, Australia, and Washington before he followed his bliss and opened a bar, the BBQ Iguana, at 14th and P, a Washington neighborhood which frequently shows up in the news about shootings, drug busts, and prostitute round-ups.

After a brush with urban terrors, Stewart moved across the Potomac River to a safer neighborhood in Arlington, Virginia, between Roslyn's high-rise jungle and Clarendon's Little Saigon where Asian restaurants were thriving. Roratonga Rodeo was Stewart's first Virginia bar that ended up as booty in a messy divorce settlement between Stewart and his wife. He moved down Wilson Boulevard and opened Amdo Rodeo which boasted 22 taps and a bar hammered from the grill of a 1973 Cadillac El Dorado. The young, hip generation that avoids Georgetown fell in love with Stewart's blend – junkyard "car art" and New Age craft beers. Stewart has his finger on the pulse of the "twentysomething" generation. They love their craft beer but just don't want to get dressed up for it. Bardo's t-shirts express their politics: No Bud No Coors No Miller No Junk.

Along his odyssey, Stewart saw a brewpub in his future. It came in the form of a boarded-up Oldsmobile dealership down the street that had given up the ghost and was on the schedule for a wrecking crew. Where others saw 24,000 sq. ft. of vacant showroom, car repair bays, and grease racks, Stewart saw acres of floor space for beer lovers to drink his beer. Beauty – or brewpub settings – are in the eye of the finder.

Bardo is a Tibetan word that refers to the 49 days after death when a body is prepared in purgatory for feeding to vultures. Stewart had spent a vacation in 1985 in Tibet where he came up with the names for his Roratonga and Amdo clubs. This Bardo period is depicted in a backroom where spare brewing equipment is kept and fluorescent murals decorate the walls. It's either a graffiti gallery or a brewery graveyard–someplace between art and a nightmare. It gives you an idea where Stewart is coming from.

Bardo boasts the largest capacity of any brewpub east of Chicago–1,200 seats, which includes the second floor recently liberated by the brooms of a cleaning crew. Stewart has been careful not to disturb the garage spirits still lurking about. Bardo's tables have wheel covers as tops and cheap plastic chairs to sit in. Music blasts from two jukeboxes: a 1968 Plymouth Fury protruding into the glassed-in showroom entrance and a 1959 Cadillac hearse in the second-floor bar. The Olmstead Oldsmobile dealer's sign still remains over the building. It probably means something.

Young Republicans love Bardo because of its dreamy, Reagan-like "life was wonderful in the '50s sort of way. Rush Limbaugh would probably show up, but it's not the place you'd expect to see Hillary and her friends. But be it Republican, Democrat, banker, lawyer, mechanic, or manicurist, everybody eventually drops by Bardo. William Kennedy Smith of Palm Beach Easter-weekend infamy, had a little fracas with a bouncer outside Bardo during the opening weeks. *USA Today*, whose offices are a few blocks away, sent reporters to interview every Bardo employee. Tabloid TV followed suit in their typical shark frenzy, and Bardo got its 15 minutes of fame.

Bardo had its problems getting the brewery running. After opening as an ale house with 37 guest beers served at 108 taps, it took almost a year until the local authorities gave Stewart a permit to brew. Stewart originally hired John Mallett, who was moonlighting from his day job at Old Dominion in Ashburn. The two parted ways in the fall of 1993 and Stewart hired Steve Allen, a homebrewer, to get his first line-up of beers going. Bardo poured its first beers in December 1993 and became Northern Virginia's first of what many expect will be a crowded field of local brewpubs. But none will likely copy Bardo. Time will tell if Stewart's formula of garage grunge brewpub has staying power.

Bardo will periodically feature beers brewed by guest brewers. The first offering was Russ' Raspberry beer, developed by Russ Scherer of Denver's Wynkoop Brewpub. Scherer was homebrewer of the year in 1985 and is a brewing legend in the West. Chang, a Tibetan beer made from gelatinized barley, will be served periodically. Bardo's food menu lists items as bizarre as Bardo's art: Hello Dalai salad, Hot Lava sandwich (hummus in pita bread). For the Vegetarian Pacifist with a Gun antipasto salad, and Atlantis, Jimmy Hoffa & Roratonga–Where are they now? grilled chicken salad.

Brewpub menu: *East Asian vegetarian dishes with a few pubfare offerings*

Russ' Raspberry beer: *brewed by Russ Scherer of Denver's Wynkoop Brewpub*

Buffalo Imperial Stout: *a medium-bodied stout with a sweet chocolate taste and a creamy head*

Chaco Canyon Chili beer: *an intense hop aroma, mild chili taste*

Slant 6 Strong Ale: *a caramel, malty tasting ale with sweet aftertaste*

Black Watch Scotch Ale

1993:   150 barrels (opened in November)

 BLUE RIDGE BREWING
709 West Main Street
Charlottesville, VA 22901   804-977-0017

Co-owners: Paul & A. Burks (Bok) Summers, Tony Conte
Brewer: Bok Summers
Equipment: 5-barrel JV Northwest system
Opened: June 1987

When Anheuser-Busch opened Busch Gardens in Williamsburg in 1969, they probably didn't realize the legislation that allowed them to open their theme park also legalized brewpubs in Virginia. Normally a conservative state reluctant to join the cultural mainstream, Virginia became open territory for anyone starting a brewpub.

Paul Summers and his brother "Bok" saw the potential for brewpub in Charlottesville. Paul was a carpenter in Charlottesville and Bok a merchant seaman with 10 years of around-the-world experience. They had been to the Manhattan Brewpub and a couple of the first California brewpubs in the mid-1980s. They were convinced the same enterprise would work in quaint Charlottesville, home of the University of Virginia which has a reputation for educating Virginia blue bloods.

The Summers brothers moved quickly and opened one of the Big East's first brewpubs, Blue Ridge Brewing, in 1987. They took over the lease of a failed restaurant, made a few renovations, and moved in with a small investment of about $250,000. They choose J.V. Northwest for their brewing equipment.

Blue Ridge Brewing is a few blocks from the University of Virginia campus in the Starr Hill neighborhood on the way downtown. Thomas Jefferson, the founder and first president of U-VA, had a bit of a reputation as a brewer himself at his home in Monticello south of town.

The Summers brothers are grandsons of Nobel Laureate William Faulkner, who taught at the University of Virginia in the 1950s. His daughter, Jill Faulkner Summers, is their mother. Co-owner Tony Conte's grandfather was a brewer with Ballantine.

The recession hurt the Charlottesville restaurant trade in the late 1980s, but Blue Ridge held on and has enjoyed an increase of business with a focus on an upscale menu and a fine dining atmosphere. This is not a campus brewpub even though it is in the shadows of U-VA. Some 75% of the clientele are Charlottesville professionals from the corporate and university administration.

Brewpub menu: *complete lunches and dinners with seafood, lamb, and local game meats; specialties are venison medallions and grilled duck breast*

Hawksbill Lager: *light golden color, mild citrus taste, soft dry finish*
Piney River Lager: *an amber lager with mild malt taste*
Afton Ale: *a light ale with faint honey and apple tones*
Sugar Hollow Heller Bock: *high alcohol, with a soft, winey texture and soft finish*
Humpback Stout: *a medium-bodied stout*

1991:   450 barrels
1992:   400 barrels
1993:   375 barreels

 LEGEND BREWING
321 West Seventh Street
Richmond, VA 23224   804-232-8871

President/Brewer: Tom Martin
Equipment: 10-barrel Bohemian system
Opened: February 1994

Tom Martin certainly has the background to open a brewpub. His father was a master brewer for Anheuser-Busch, and Tom graduated from the University of California at Davis brewing program. Tom worked for Anheuser-Busch in Tampa for a few years and also at their brewery in Williamsburg, VA. His 15-year dream to have his own brewery became a reality in February 1994 when his Legend Brewery opened.

Legend is in an industrial area on the banks of the James River across from downtown, in Richmond's financial district. Martin's father assists as a consultant for his son's brewery.

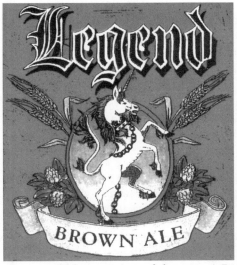

Legend is one of the tiniest brewpubs in the country with four stools at the bar and one table squeezed into an L-shaped corner at the entrance. The fire code allows only 15 people in the brewery at one time, but the crowds that show up for tours on Saturday exceed that number with the first cars that show up. Martin believes that the crowds Legend has attracted the first few months of operations is a hint of the potential for a restaurant he wants to open in the adjoining facility he has already leased. The restaurant patio would have a view of downtown Richmond across the river.

The Legend's logo is a unicorn from Scottish heraldry that Tom studied when he ran a gift shop in colonial Williamsburg. The unicorn came from the Scottish heraldry of James III, who became James I of England. When James's English heraldry was designed, one of the unicorns from his original Scottish banner was replaced by a lion. Martin chose the "missing unicorn" as his logo for Legend. The James River, named after King James, runs through Richmond and separates the town from the Legend brewery.

Legend's beers are available on draft in the key Richmond areas in the Fan, Shockoe Slip, Shockoe Bottom, and South Side restaurants.

Brewpub menu: *pubfare*

Legend Lager: *a light lager, with a crisp, clean taste*
Legend Pilsener: *a big pilsener in the continental style*
Legend Brown Ale: *a medium-bodied English-style brown ale*
Legend Porter: *a well-balanced, creamy porter with a rich malty taste and mild licorice notes*

≋ OLD DOMINION BREWING
44633 Guilford Drive #112
Ashburn, VA 22011   162703-689-1225

President: Jerry Bailey
Brewers: John Mallett and Ron Barchet
Equipment: 25-barrel JV Northwest system with Krones bottling line
Opened: May 1990

Jerry Bailey was a Foreign Service officer in his 50s with the Agency for International Development (AID) when he grew disenchanted with the prospects of retiring as a government worker. He started homebrewing in Bethesda and began considering opening a brewery. When he became serious in the mid-1980s, he went to the Stoudt Brewery in Adamstown, PA, and paid Ed and Carol Stoudt to teach him how to brew their award-winning beer.

Bailey raised $1 million from family, friends, and investors and found a site 25 miles from downtown Washington, D.C., in a new industrial park in Virginia's Loudon County. The location is in the high-tech corridor near Dulles Airport where, on a clear day, the Blue Ridge Mountains to the west provide a scenic backdrop. Loudon County is making a rapid conversion from sleepy horse country and dairy farms to congested but well-manicured subdivisions and shopping centers.

Old Dominion filled a need for a high-quality craft brewery in the Washington area that surprisingly had not developed much of a brewing presence with the exception of contract-brewed Olde Heurich in Washington and the ill-fated Virginia Brewing (formerly Chesbay) in Norfolk, which went bankrupt in 1992.

In addition to several of its own brands, Old Dominion brews for Washington-area restaurants and private accounts including Victory Amber, Murphy's, Old Dubliner, Aviator Amber, Blue Point, Hard Times Select, Virginia Native, O'Bannon's Dark, and St. George. Two of these premium accounts are Clyde's and Hard Times Cafe, which had been brewed by Virginia Brewing before they went out of business. They also picked up the brewing assignment for the prestigious colonial Williamsburg King's Arms Tavern.

One of the most charming aspects of Old Dominion are its traditional Saturday tours. At 12 and 3 PM, Jerry leads groups of 80 around the brewery and, with his typically droll, self-effacing manner, makes friends of everyone who comes. A free beer or two in the hospitality suite (which is the office during the week) doesn't hurt.

Bailey is a well-known and popular figure in Washington's brewing community. He is so tolerant that he allowed brewer John Mallett to moonlight at Bardo Rodeo as the Arlington brewpub was weaving its way through the hazardous permitting and startup period.

The story of Old Dominion is one of a rapidly maturing craft brewery. From its initial offerings of a standard ale and lager, Bailey guided the brewery to produce an Oktoberfest beer, holiday beer, wheat beer, and barley wine. Old Dominion's root beer is also a big seller in restaurants, grocery stores, and supermarkets all over Washington. Their success has put them on a rigorous brewing schedule brewing 3 times a day with 2 brews on Saturdays. If that doesn't make them busy enough, Bailey is seriously considering putting in a small brewpub in a 200 sq. ft. "corner" in the brewery for the tours and weekend business. The pub would feature the 14 beers Old Dominion brews for themselves and private accounts.

Old Dominion's rapid growth has put them in a constant state of expansion. Since opening in 1990, the brewery has grown from less than 3,000 barrels a year to a projected 18,000–20,000 barrels in 1994. Their location in an underutilized industrial park and the departure of a neighboring tenant allowed Old Dominion to expand with eight new 100-barrel fermentors and storage tanks in 1994. With such growth, they could become a 100,000 barrel brewery before they know it. Look for Old Dominion to become a major player on the East Coast in years to come.

Dominion Lager: *brewed with two-row, Munich, dextrin, and caramel malts; Clusters and Hallertau bittering hops and Tettnang, Hallertau, Hersbrucker, and Saaz aromatic hops*
Dominion Ale: *a medium-bodied, lightly hopped American ale brewed with two-row pale, caramel, and black malts; Clusters, Willamette, and Mt. Hood hops*
Dominion Helles: *a light in color and body German style brewed with Munich and two-row malts, Hallertau and Hersbrucker hops*
Dominion Stout: *a creamy Irish-style cream stout; soft and mellow with warm, coffee aftertaste*
Holiday Ale: *a strong red ale*

1991:   3,389 barrels
1992:   6,092 barrels
1993:   10,225 barrels

POTOMAC RIVER BREWING
14141-A Parke Long Court
Chantilly, VA 22021   703-631-5430

President: Jerry Russell
Brewer: Chris Schwartz
Equipment: 20-barrel JV Northwest system from Bridgeport Brewery in Portland, Oregon
Opened: September 1993

Jerry Russell, a former Navy officer, opened northern Virginia's second craft brewery in 1993, after seeing the success of Old Dominion in nearby Ashburn. He had been homebrewing for several years and visiting brewpubs on the West Coast when he traveled.

After he retired from the Navy, Russell worked as a government contractor until he had the resources and a business plan to start his own brewery. His plan was to brew ales like he had found on the West Coast. He took an intensive brewing course at the Siebel Institute in Chicago to enhance his skills as a brewer.

Russell purchased Portland's Bridgeport Brewery's original equipment for less than $80,000 and shipped it across country via rail. He spent the spring and summer of 1993 installing the equipment in an industrial area near Dulles Airport in affluent Fairfax County. Even though he had skills as a brewer, Russell hired Chris Schwartz, who formerly brewed at McGuire's Brewpub in Pensacola. Schwartz is also a Navy man, having been stationed at Pensacola's Naval Air Station.

The brewery's single beer, Patowmack Ale, is named after the native Americans who had settled in the woods and lowlands along the river before Pierre L'Enfant and Thomas Jefferson showed up with plans for a capital city.

Patowmack Ale is available on draft at about a dozen restaurants in the Virginia suburbs. Russell plans to add a bottling line and come up with a second beer, probably a porter, in 1994. His wife, Sharon, takes care of the books for the brewery.

Patowmack Ale: *a medium-bodied, copper-colored pale ale brewed with two-row barley, caramel malt, Cascade and Mt. Hood hops; a smooth, well-balanced ale with a smooth mouthfeel and a crisp dry finish*

1993:   N/A (opened in September)

RICHBRAU BREWERY
1214 E. Cary Street
Richmond, VA 23219   804-644-3018

Co-owners: David McGil and Graham Ramsay
Brewer: John Hallberg
Equipment: 14-barrel Pub Brewing system
Opened: July 1993

The Richbrau Brewery is in the historic Shockoe Slip in Richmond's bottom lands along the James River. The area was the home of tobacco and liquor warehouses constructed in the 1830s and burned down April 2, 1865, as Union troops advanced on the Confederate Capital. The Shockoe Slip was rebuilt during 1868–88 as a tobacco warehouse and mercantile area. It was declared a historic preservation area and now is alive with popular restaurants, saloons, shops, and office space. Shockoe Slip's cobblestoned streets have been smoothed over by more than a century of wagon, horse, car, and pedestrian traffic. Electrified gas lamps reminiscent of the 19th-century fixtures light the streets at night.

The Richbrau Brewery is co-located with the Queens Arms Pub on Cary Street, the main thoroughfare of Shockoe Slip. The brewery is located in a building built in the 1820s on three floors of the building with the grain mill on the third floor, the brewhouse on the bottom floor, and the fermentation tanks on the second floor. The overall look is one of a dusty saloon with worn wooden fixtures, old fireplace, and creaky stairs to the second floor game area. Close your eyes and you can imagine a Confederate officer and his lady strolling in for a refreshing drink on a hot July afternoon.

A few blocks away is the State Capitol, the second oldest capitol in the country, and Capital of the Confederacy, the Museum and White House of the Confederacy, and St. John's Church where Patrick Henry gave his "Give me liberty or give me death" speech at the Second Virginia Convention on March 23, 1775.

Brewer John Hallberg took brewing courses at the Siebel Institute in Chicago and the University of California at Davis. He brewed at Old Dominion Brewery and a couple of Washington-area breweries before starting at Richbrau in 1993.

Richbrau recently received permission to sell their beer in growlers and to local restaurants. The brewpub jumps with local rock and country bands Thursday through Saturday nights.

Brewpub menu: *pubfare with a few southern specialties; red beans and rice and crawfish étouffeé*

Old Nick Pale Ale: *an amber-colored ale with mellow, smooth malty taste*
Golden Griffin Ale: *a light golden-colored ale with a slight lemony taste*
Big Nasty Porter: *ebony-colored porter with a slight coffee aftertaste*
Poe's Tell Tale Ale: *a light-bodied barley wine with a mild toffee aftertaste; named after the poet Edgar Allen Poe, who once lived a few blocks away*

1993:   400 barrels (opened in July)

CAPITOL CITY BREWERY

1100 New York Avenue NW
Washington, DC 20005   202-628-2222

Co-owners: Jack Keniley, David von Storch, Bill Foster
Brewer: Martin Virga
Equipment: 14-barrel used JV Northwest system
Opened: August 1992

Washington has been a thirsty place since the Heurich Brewery closed in 1956. Grandson Gary revived the family brewery via a contract operation in 1987, but the nation's capital didn't have a living, breathing brewery until Capitol City opened in 1992. Washington's first brewpub opened in the old Greyhound bus depot across from the Convention Center and high-priced hotels. Within days it had attracted crowds that have made its success legendary among local restaurateurs and beer lovers. With its success, it's a wonder that no one else had moved in to take advantage of Capitol City's good fortune.

Capitol City's neo-industrial motif is more what one might expect from a city like Cleveland, Pittsburgh, or Chicago where they do real work. But Washington is a city whose economy runs to politics and pâté, not shipping docks and assembly lines. Nevertheless, Capitol City comes with exposed girders, catwalks, electrical trays, and a brew kettle behind the bar. But the brew kettle is a eunuch, designed for show and never to take part in the joys of brewing

Pedestrians can gaze at the happy throngs inside Capitol City from the intersection of New York Avenue and 11th Street. The brewpub's crowds have more than a little to do with its location across the street from the Convention Center and two major hotels. If that's not enough, Capitol City has developed a following from Washington's "power lunch" club of lobbyists, lawyers, and government workers and the normal throngs of tourists, singles, and beer lovers who want to be where the action is.

Brewer Martin Virga may seem a little misplaced at an urban brewpub. He worked at the Kaiser Brau Brewery in Bavaria and studied for two years at Doemens Technical School in Munich. His training prepared him to brew classic German styles which age in storage tanks – not the brewpub ales which are rushed to be served in a few days. Nevertheless,

Virga produces German Kolsch and Altbiers along with more conventional English ales and porters found in the majority of brewpubs.

Capitol City has had a problem keeping beer in its tanks since its opening in August 1992. Its capacity is 1,800 barrels a year but it sells about three times that much. Fortunately, the Washington area has three craft breweries to pick up the slack: Oxford and Wild Goose in Maryland and Old Dominion in Virginia. Oxford's Eleanor Amber is the most popular beer in the brewpub, selling 40 kegs a week. Capitol City's management says future plans call for an off-site brewery to meet the demand.

Brewpub menu: *complete lunches and dinners from burgers and chili to crab cakes and grilled seafood*

Pale Ale: *a medium-bodied, well-balanced amber ale*
Bitter
Porter
Nut Brown Ale: *a slightly sweet, light-bodied brown ale with a hint of nutty caramel*
Kolsch: *a top-fermented German style from Cologne; brewed with Saaz hops and wheat malt*
Stout
Altbier: *brewed with two-row Vienna and Munich malts: Hallertau, Northern Brewer, and Hersbrucker-Perle hops and ale yeast*

1992:   1,200 barrels
1993:   1,200 barrels

 OLDE HEURICH BREWING COMPANY
3323 M Street NW
Washington, DC 20007   202-333-2313

President: Gary Heurich
Brewer: Contract brewed at F. X. Matt Brewery, Utica, NY
Opened: June 1986

The Heurich Brewery was Washingon's largest and the longest lasting brewery in the nation's capital. It's colorful history centers on the founder, Christian Heurich, who emigrated to the U.S. in 1876 from his native Bavaria. He had traveled around Germany working in breweries as a youngster and realized his future was more promising in America than in Bismarckian Germany.

When Heurich arrived in the U.S. in 1876, he lived with his sister in Baltimore, a city that had many German breweries. He moved to Washington and worked in a tavern until he bought his first brewery/tavern near Dupont Circle. Today we would call the place a brewpub. Heurich relocated in 1889 to waterfront property on the Potomac River known as Foggy Bottom because of the miasma that rose daily from the lowland swamp.

 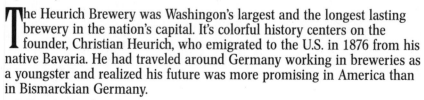

Heurich's built a massive granite brewery on the site that stood as a landmark even before the Jefferson Memorial was built or Memorial Bridge constructed.

Christian Heurich went to his brewery every day until the last two weeks he was alive. He died in 1945 at the age of 102 in the family mansion one block from Dupont Circle. The family mansion is now home of

the Columbia Historical Society (2231 New Hampshire Avenue), with library, archives, and photo collection of the early history of Washington. Tours are offered daily of the grand old mansion, which is one of the most cherished private museums in the city. Heurich hired German craftsmen, brought wood from Germany, and built it in the style of a Barvarian landholder's estate. They just don't do it this well anymore.

Heurich's son, Christian, Jr., ran the brewery until 1956, when it closed. The city demolished the brewery in 1962 to make way for the Roosevelt Bridge, Watergate Hotel, and the Kennedy Center for the Performing Arts. Not a bad legacy for a classic old brewery–replaced by historical landmarks and a palace of arts.

Grandson Gary revived the family's brewing tradition in 1986 when he was only 26. He designed a label to emphasize the family's heritage with the nation's capital and focused his market in Washington, Maryland, and Virginia.

The original name of Old Heurich Amber Lager was changed to Maerzen in recognition of the style of beer it truly was. Gary has always said he would build a brewery or brewpub in the Washington area and is studying a site in suburban Maryland as a brewpub location, He is contemplating brewing a second beer, a European pilsener, in 1994. Olde Heurich is brewed on contract at the F. X. Matt Brewery in Utica, NY.

Olde Heurich Maerzen: *a deep amber-colored lager with spicy floral aroma, creamy head and smooth, malty aftertaste*

1991: 2,089 barrels
1992: 3,751 barrrels
1993: N/A

South

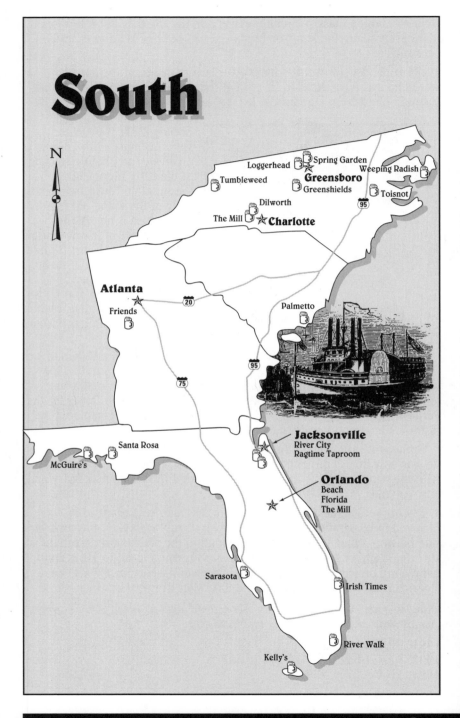

N

Loggerhead Spring Garden
Tumbleweed Weeping Radish
Greensboro
Greenshields Toisnot

Dilworth
The Mill **Charlotte**

95

Atlanta
Friends

20

Palmetto

95

75

Santa Rosa

McGuire's

Jacksonville
River City
Ragtime Taproom

Orlando
Beach
Florida
The Mill

Sarasota

Irish Times

River Walk

Kelly's

BEACH BREWING
5905 S. Kirkman Road
Orlando, FL 32819   407-345-8802

President: Angela Ranson
Brewer: Brian Baldasano
Equipment: 10-barrel JV Northwest system
Opened: June 1992

Beach is Florida's first craft brewery not attached to a brewpub. Nevertheless, it does brew for the Mill Brewery, Bakery, and Eatery restaurants in Tallahassee, Gainesville, and Orlando, which were formerly brewpubs. Beach is located in the front of the Orlando Mill, which originally opened in 1988 as the Winter Park Brewing Company.

Beach also brews for some well-known accounts – Disney World and the Orlando Cubs minor league team – and some central Florida restaurant chains.

Beach's flagship beer, Honey Wheat Light, has won awards at Florida beer festivals since it was first introduced in 1992.

Honey Wheat Light: *brewed with honey and wheat*
Magic Brew: *an amber*
Red Rock: *a nut brown ale*

1992:   328 barrels
1993:   750 barrels

 ## FLORIDA BEER BRANDS
645 W. Michigan Street
Orlando, FL 32805   800-741-BREW

President: Bill Burrer
Brewer/Equipment: Contract brewed at August Schell Brewery
Opened: 1988

Two Florida entrepreneurs, Bill Burrer and Chip Weston, had worked on a greeting card project in the 1970s and developed a good working relationship. Burrer was on the marketing side of the business, and Weston did the art and design work. When Burrer got the idea to move into the craft beer industry in 1987, the two of them came up with a concept to sell beer and brewery merchandise based upon romantic American legends. Their company, Florida Beer Brands, has three product lines featuring western cowboys, Florida alligators, and American fliers during World War II.

Florida's Gator Lager was introduced in 1989 and features the lore of Florida's alligators. The beer is packaged in green bottles with cartoon images of an alligator in sunglasses holding a cold one.

In May 1993, Florida Brands introduced its line of Old West beers evoking the romantic era of the old cowboy outlaws – Jesse James, Butch Cassidy and the Sundance Kid, Billy the Kid, Calamity Jane, and Bat Masterson. Florida's Old West labels feature 20 prints of these western legends in period piece artwork.

The Flying Aces lineup is a testimony of the heroism of World War II American fliers who painted the noses of their fighters and bombers with painted ladies, birds, animals, fish, and whatever evoked their spirit or warrior fantasy. By the time all the labels are approved and printed, there will be 15 images of the old fighters.

Burrer brews his beer on contract at the August Schell Brewery in New Ulm, Minnesota. Their literature claims that New Ulm was burned during the 1862 Sioux Uprising, but the brewery was left intact because of the owner's friendship with the local Indians. They haven't found alligators in any of the lakes around New Ulm yet, and the only planes seen around that part of Minnesota are crop dusters.

At the 1993 Great American Beer Festival, Old West Amber beer won the gold medal in the category usually reserved for Boston Beer's Samuel Adams, whose Oktoberfest had to settle for the silver medal. Burrer says he spent more than two years developing the recipe for his award winning amber beer. Florida Beer Brands sells brewery-related merchandise with gift catalogs and an 800 number. Their beers are sold in 20 states and three foreign countries.

Florida Brand's next beer will be Black Alligator, expected to roll out in 16-oz. bottles in 1994. The beer will be a black lager brewed at August Schell. Burrer says that alligators are actually black, not green, which is a common misperception about the state's favorite reptile.

Gator Lager
Gator Lager Light
Old West Amber: *winner of gold medal for amber beer at 1993 Great American Beer Festival*
Old West Light: *the same recipe as Gator Lager Light*
Flying Aces Light: *the same recipe as Gator Lager Light*

1992:   653 barrels
1993:   N/A

IRISH TIMES BREWERY
9920 Alternate A1A, Promenade Plaza
Palm Beach Gardens, FL 33410   407-624-1504

Owners: Alan & Hillary Craig
Brewer: Flip Gary
Equipment: 7-barrel Pub system
Opened: 1991

Irish Times is another one of Florida's numerous neighborhood pubs for customers nostalgic about their vacations to the United Kingdom. The interior has the rustic country pub look with brick walls, brass rails and fixtures, and Irish memorabilia all around.

Irish Time's menu relates traditional blarney about Irish customs and legends, in particular the one of Finn MacCool, a third-century warrior in the court of the High King. According to legend, Finn recovered treasure by slaying a dragon, ate a salmon giving him wisdom and courage, built the Giants Causeway in County Antrim, and tossed a piece of land into the Irish sea creating the Isle of Man. He is such a worthy soul that Irish Times honored him by naming their beers after him.

Irish Time's menu has traditional Irish offerings with every course. Desserts are Bailey's Irish Cream Pie, apple tart, and tricolor pie. Harp, Guinness, and Bass Ale are on tap. A recent expansion increased capacity from 140 to 210 seats.

Brewer Flip Gary also handles the brewing chores at Kelly's Caribbean Brewery and Grill in Key West, where he brews twice a week.

Brewpub menu: *Irish pubfare and specialities: corned beef, malt fries, beef & Guinness pie, Shepherd's pie, bangers & mash, Irish stew, corned beef & cabbage*

Mac Red: *a brown ale*
Mac Lite: *a wheat beer*
Mac Pale: *a pale ale*
Mac Berry: *a wheat ale brewed with raspberries*

1991:   **400 barrels**
1992:   **N/A**
1993:   **400 barrels**

 ## KELLY'S/SOUTHERNMOST BREWERY
301 Whitehead Street
Key West, FL 33041   305-293-8484

Co-owners: Kelly McGillis & Fred Tillman
Brewer: Flip Gary
Equipment: 7-barrel Century system

Opened: May 1993

Actress Kelly McGillis of *Witness* fame and husband Fred Tillman have opened the Southernmost Brewery in the country's southernmost city of Key West. Tillman is a Florida restauranteur looking to start a chain of brewpubs on the East Coast.

Southernmost's theme is the clipper ship era when Pan American flew daily to Havana from Key West. Kelly's Caribbean Bar and Grill is located in the same building, a block off Duval Street, Key West's main street.

Patrons can enjoy the balmy sea breezes on the deck and in the gardens. Inside is an art gallery, a library of Key West's expatriate writers following their Hemingway muse, and a museum with Pan Am memorabilia.

Brewpub menu: *seafood and Caribbean dishes: pasta with shrimp and lime, fresh fish with papaya and toasted coconut*

Key West Golden Ale
Havana Red Ale
Paradiso Caribe Beer Color
Southern Clipper
Black Bart's Root Beer

1993: 258 barrels

 ## MCGUIRE'S IRISH PUB
600 East Gregory Street
Pensacola, FL 32501   904-433-6789

President: McGuire Martin
Brewer: Steve Fried
Equipment: 6-barrel locally designed system
Opened: February 3, 1989

What was started by McGuire and Molly Martin as a small liquor store and Irish pub in 1977 has grown, in less than two decades, into one of the most successful Irish pubs and brewpubs in the country.

McGuire Martin's introduction to Irish pub life was his grandmother's saloon in Philadelphia, where he grew up and his father's steak house in southern New Jersey. After graduating from Vanderbilt University with a degree in business administration, McGuire worked for Sheraton Hotels and Saga Food Service and had his own dietary management business for hospitals and colleges in the South.

McGuire and his wife, Molly, struck out on their own when they took over a small liquor store in Pensacola and made it into an Irish pub. In 1982, McGuire's moved to its present Gregory Street location in Pensacola's original firehouse.

Tradition is the key to McGuire's success. Its most famous tradition is that of having customers sign their name to a dollar bill, date it, and tack it to the ceiling. What started as a lark by Molly, who tacked her first $1 tip to the back bar, has now grown into a collection of more than $90,000 momentos of patrons' visits!

McGuire's autographed dollar bills include those signed by movie stars (Brooke Shields), rock stars (David Bowie), boxers (Larry Holmes), singers (Janet Jackson), and Vice Presidents (Al Gore). McGuire's pays income taxes on the dollar bills and includes it as a business asset of the pub. Fire insurance, unfortunately, won't insure the momentos.

More than 5,000 of McGuire's regulars also have their own personalized mugs for their use when they stop by. Cartoonist Jeff MacNelly liked McGuire's so much he drew a cartoon of his famous "Shoe" at McGuire's for a T-shirt that is a best seller in the gift shop.

Brewer Steve Fried was a local homebrewer who read McGuire's ad for a brewer in the local paper. He applied, got the job, and apprenticed with Rush Cummings of Louisiana's Abita Brewing. Cummings also helped design McGuire's brewing system, which was built by a local contractor who did McGuire's refrigeration work.

In addition to his regular beers, Fried plans to brew an Irish Cream Ale, raspberry wheat, shandy (lemonade and beer), brown ale, and an Oktoberfest. The Oldenberg Brewery in Kentucky brews and bottles Irish Old Style Ale for McGuire's off-premise trade.

Irish Red: *McGuire's most popular beer; half of the brewery's production*
McGuire's Lite
Porter
Stout
Christmas ale
Barley wine

1991:   800 barrels
1992:   800 barrels
1993:   800 barrels

MILL BREWERY, BAKERY, AND EATERY
30 West Fairbanks Avenue
Winter Park, FL 32789   407-644-1544

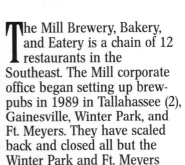

President: Paul Smith
Brewer: John Stuart
Equipment: 7-barrel JV Northwest system
Opened: 1989

The Mill Brewery, Bakery, and Eatery is a chain of 12 restaurants in the Southeast. The Mill corporate office began setting up brew-pubs in 1989 in Tallahassee (2), Gainesville, Winter Park, and Ft. Meyers. They have scaled back and closed all but the Winter Park and Ft. Meyers branches.

Paul Smith visited brewpubs in California, Colorado, Oregon, and Washington and believed the concept would work in his Mill Bakery and Eatery chain. He hired consultant Karl Strauss to set up his breweries and come up with recipes.

Brewer John Stuart started at the N. Monroe Tallahassee Mill but moved to Winter Park when the brewery was closed in Tallahassee. Before he joined the Mill organization, Stuart worked at two early Texas craft breweries: Reinheitsbebot in Plano, and Addison Brewing in Addison. A long time homebrewer, Stuart is active with the Central Florida Homebrewers Club.

Beach Brewing Company in Orlando brews for the Mills that have closed their brewing operations. Fresh breads and pastries are baked at the Mills.

Brewpub menu: *complete breakfasts, lunches, and dinners; seafood, pizza, and pasta specialties*

Big Cypress: *an India pale ale*
Pelican Gold: *a light lager*
Honey Wheat: *a wheat beer brewed with orange blossom honey*
Magic Brew: *a nut brown ale brewed in honor of the Orlando Magic NBA team*
Red Rock: *an amber ale*

1992:   1,000 barrels
1993:   730 barrels

RAGTIME TAPROOM
207 Atlantic Boulevard
Atlantic Beach, FL 32233   904-241-7877

Co-owners: Bill & Tom Morton
Brewer: Scott Morton
Equipment: 10-barrel BRD system
Opened: September 1991

Bill and Tom Morton operated the popular Ragtime Tavern on Florida's Atlantic coastline for 10 years before they added a brewery and became a brewpub. They hired a third brother, Scott, to brew for them.

Ragtime's owners were clever to select the name Red Brick Ale for one of their beers. They claim it refers to the interior of their brewpub and not the name of a small press publishing books about craft breweries. But it's a nice coincidence. Ragtime also put their Red Brick Ale label on a t-shirt. Every craft brew lover should have one.

A. Strange stout is named after the owners' grandfather, Alexander Strange, who, as a youth, helped his grandfather deliver Whitbread Ale to Glasgow pubs.

Brewpub menu: *seafood and cajun specialties*

Red Brick Ale
A. Strange Stout
Westbury Wheat
Dolphins Breath Lager

1991:   **316 barrels** (opened in September)
1992:   **1,600 barrels**
1993:   **1,500 barrels**

RIVER CITY BREWING
835 Gulf Life Drive
Jacksonville, FL 32207   904-398-2299

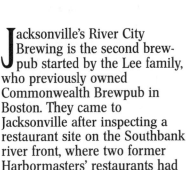

Co-owners: Jim & Jeff Lee
Brewers: Dan Kramer and Steve Sullivan
Equipment: 10-barrel Pub Brewing system
Opened: November 5, 1993

Jacksonville's River City Brewing is the second brewpub started by the Lee family, who previously owned Commonwealth Brewpub in Boston. They came to Jacksonville after inspecting a restaurant site on the Southbank river front, where two former Harbormasters' restaurants had failed, leaving the city with a debt of nearly $3 million in a guaranteed federal loan.

The Lees spent $1 million renovating the restaurant into a brewpub and opened in November 1993. In the first four months of operation, River City's gross sales were almost $2 million, which projects to $6 million in sales the first year. River City's theme is English nautical with racing shells, masts, spars, antiques, sails, and ship models. River City has the capacity to brew 1,500 barrels/year. Authentic beer engines are being imported from England to serve cask-conditioned ales.

Several of the management staff at River City came down with the Lee family to open the brewpub. Dan Kramer and Steve Sullivan both brewed in Boston at Commonwealth. Boston is the most dynamic brewing city on the East Coast. Florida is trying to catch up, at least in the number of brewpubs. The challenge for the River City crew will be to brew distinctive beers like those found in New England, without watering them down to satisfy newcomers to the beer culture.

Chefs Tim and Barbara Felver had previously worked at one of Jacksonville's top restaurants, 24 Miramar. Barbara's specialty is desserts – her crème brulée is a local favorite. River City Brewing is Jacksonville's second brewpub; Ragtime Tavern and Tap Room in Atlantic Beach was the first.

Brewpub menu: *complete lunches and dinners with seafood, southern, cajun, and pasta specialties*

Jag Light
Red Rooster
Jackson Pale Ale
Riptide Porter

1993: (opened in November)

RIVER WALK BREWERY
111 SW 2nd Avenue
Fort Lauderdale, FL 33301   305-764-8448

President: Chris Stasinos
Brewer: Mark Safarik
Equipment: 10-barrel HBH system from Germany; fermenters from Pub Brewing
Opened: 1991

River Walk is Ft. Lauderdale's first brewpub and one of the first on Florida's Atlantic coast.

Brewer Mark Safarik had brewed in three California brewpubs in the early 1990s: State Street in Santa Barbara, Manhattan Beach in Manhattan Beach, and Pacific Tap and Grill in San Rafael. He made the move to Florida in January 1994 to work for River Walk. One of his first assignments was to upgrade and redesign the brewing equipment to improve production.

Brewpub menu: *pubfare with steak and seafood specialities*

Marlin's Light
White Tip Wheat
Blackbeard's Gold
Riverwalk Red
Panther's Porter
Black Marlin Oatmeal Stout

SANTA ROSA BREWING
54 Miracle Strip Parkway SE
Fort Walton Beach, FL 32548   904-664-2739

President:
Theodore Bass
Brewer:
Equipment: 10-barrel Century
system
Opened: November 1992

The Santa Rosa Brewery is in a seaside restaurant in Ft. Walton Beach, a resort community near Pensacola and the Pensacola Naval Air Station.

Brewpub menu: *steak, seafood, and Mexican dishes*

Wheat Beer
Ice Beer
Honey Beer

1992:   (opened in November)
1993:   1,500 barrels

SARASOTA BREWING
6607 Gateway Ave.
Sarasota, FL 34231   813-925-2337

Owners: Gil & Jeff Rosenberg
Brewer: Andy Rathmann
Equipment: 7-barrel JV Northwest system
Opened: September 1989

Sarasota is the first brewpub on Florida's Gulf Coast, located on Sarasota's Siesta Key.

The father and son team of Gil and Jeff Rosenberg opened Sarasota Brewing in 1989 and followed with a second brewpub in Bradenton in 1991.

Brewer Andy Rathmann had worked as an electrical engineer in the defense industry and traveled extensively throughout the

U.S., Europe, and the Middle East. When the Cold War ended, Rathmann was looking around for a new field in which to use his technical skills and have a little fun.

Rathmann was living in Germany and applied to the prestigious Weihenstephan Technical Brewing Institute. But he was turned down because he didn't have the necessary technical experience, so he went to work in three German breweries to get experience. Germany has an apprenticeship tradition which requires a worker to spend time in various fields before being promoted or becoming eligible for schooling.

Rathmann eventually studied at the University of California at Davis and received his masterbrewer certificate in 1993 from the Institute of Brewing in London.

Brewpub menu: *pubfare*

Cobra Lite
Sequoia Amber
Original Prague Pilsner
Pelicanator Double Bock
Full Moon Maibock
Blue Marlin Marzen
Presidential Pale Ale
Sara Desota Golden Ale
Queens Porter
Ya Mills Honeymead Ale
Christmas Cream Ale Special

1993:   550 barrels

FRIENDS BREWERY
P.O. Box 29464
Atlanta, GA 30359   404-325-1235

Owners: Dow Scoggins, Frank Cronin, Phil Churchman, Rick Roberts, & Jon Downing
Brewer: Jon Downing
Equipment: Contract brewed at August Schell Brewery in Minnesota
Opened: 1988

Friends Brewing is actually that, a group of friends who all are graduates of Georgia State University joined in a partnership to open a brewery. Dow Scoggins, the leader behind the venture, is a former systems engineer who left his job in 1988 to visit craft breweries and develop a business plan. He worked in the Catamount Brewery in Vermont and the Wheatley Brewery in Ontario to learn commercial brewing.

While traveling in Canada, Scoggins met Jon Downing, the brewer at the Simcoe Brewery in Ontario. Downing is a seasoned brewer with experience in Canada, England, and the U.S. A graduate of the U.S. Brewers Academy in Chicago, Downing has worked as a consultant setting up breweries in Russia, Ukraine, and the Caribbean.

The original Helenboch Brewery opened in 1990 in Helen, 80 miles north of Atlanta, in the Appalachian Mountains. The brewery was closed with plans to reopen in Atlanta where the market for Hellenboch beers is greatest. Helenboch is now brewed on contract in New Ulm, Minnesota at the August Schell Brewery.

Friend's newest product is a Georgia peach wheat beer using fresh Georgia peaches. A beer made with Georgia's other well-known product, peanuts, was considered but peanuts don't ferment well. Jimmy would have loved it.

Helenboch beer: *a helles style beer, brewed with Munich, pale, and carapils malts and Saaz and Hallterau hops; silver medal winner in Munchner category at the 1989 Great American Beer Festival*
Helenboch Oktoberfest: *gold medal winner in the European Dark/Munchner Dunkel style at 1991 Great American Beer Festival*

Georgia Peach Wheat: *brewed with 50% malted barley and 50% malted wheat, Cascade and Hallertau hops, and a dash of peach flavor*

1991: 700 barrels
1992: 550 barrels
1993: 800 barrels

DILWORTH BREWING

1301 East Blvd.
Charlotte, NC 28203   704-377-2739

Co-owners: John Begley, Ed Collins, Bob Binnion
Brewer: Ed Collins
Equipment: 7-barrel JV Northwest and 10-barrel Century system
Opened: March 1988

Dilworth Brewing was the first brewery to open in Charlotte since the Atlantic Brewery closed in 1956. It was the second North Carolina brewpub after Weeping Radish opened in Manteo in 1987. The original operation went out of business and three new partners bought it and reopened in 1990. John Begley had a background in the restaurant business, and Ed Collins was a graduate of the Siebel Institute.

With a population of approximately 750,000, Charlotte is emerging as a growing financial center in the South, with a number of banking concerns and a high profile in national sports. The NFL awarded an expansion team to Charlotte after seeing the local support for the NBA Charlotte Hornets. The major college in town is a branch of the University of North Carolina, UNC-Charlotte.

The Brew Pub Poets Society meets at the Dilworth brewpub to discuss light verse and craft beers. The members' more distinguished contributions are framed and hang on the walls of the brewpub. Live music is featured from Wednesday to Saturday night. The brewpub is located five minutes from downtown in the historic Dilworth neighborhood.

A new 10-barrel brewery at Dilworth started brewing in February, 1994. The expansion will allow Dilworth to sell 12-oz. bottles and half-barrel kegs for off premise restaurant trade in Charlotte, Greensboro, Raleigh, and Durham. The capacity for the new brewing system is 6,000 barrels per year.

Brewpub menu: *pubfare*

Latta Light
Reed's Gold Pilsner

Albemarle Ale: *bronze medal winner in amber ale category at the 1992 Great American Beer Festival*
Dilworth Porter

1991:   650 barrels
1992:   900 barrels
1993:   1,200 barrels

〰 GREENSHIELDS BREWERY
214 East Martin Street
Raleigh, NC 27601   919-829-0214

Co-owners: Gary & Martha Greenshields
Brewer: Gary Greenshields
Equipment: 20-barrel German brew house
Opened: July 6, 1989

Gary Greenshields had a sterling corporate background having worked for 25 years for some of America's giant companies – Falstaff, Anheuser-Busch, and R.J. Reynolds. With a B.A. in chemistry and an MBA, Greenshields learned marketing, product development, niche products, and small business acquisition. After two decades with big business, he wanted to put his experience to work for himself. He had watched the craft brewing industry emerge in the early 1980s and felt that, with his background in the brewing and restaurant business, he could find a place to be his own boss.

Gary and his wife, Martha, visited East Coast brewpubs and flew to England to study pubs. The lesson they learned was that pubs' success was based on a combination of fresh-tasting beer and a pleasant, casual atmosphere where families and friends could gather. English pubs have been doing that quite well for centuries. The Greenshields wanted to create the same formula in an American setting.

Gary and Martha went to work writing a business plan and raising about $1 million to build a brewpub in North Carolina's Research Triangle. They selected Raleigh's historic City Market, which was formerly a farmers' market, and opened in July 1989. The ambiance is casual but comfortable, with sofas, dark woods, and elegant furnishings.

Greenshields has three floors for casual dining, relaxing at the bar or near the fireplace, or sitting outside in the beer garden. An expansion planned for 1994 will allow for a more spacious beer garden, an English country pub room, more fireplaces, and a new German 20-barrel brewhouse. Capacity with the new brewhouse will allow for producing 7,000 barrels/year.

The Greenshields Brewery is truly a family operation. Gary works on the brewing and day-to-day operations, Martha takes care of administrative details, a daughter is in charge of bookkeeping and finances, and a son-in-law is the restaurant manager. The family plans on opening more Greenshields Brewpubs when time – and money – allow.

Brewpub menu: *complete lunches and dinners with English family pub specialties*

Greenshield's Amber
Greenshield's India Pale Ale

1991:   1,000 barrels
1992:   1,171 barrels
1993:   1,190 barrels

 LOGGERHEAD BREWING
2006 W. Vandalia Road
Greensboro, NC 27407   919-292-7676

President: Gary Vickers
Brewer: Larry Stanley
Equipment: 7-barrel JV Northwest system
Opened: April 1990

Co-owners Gary Vickers and Larry Stanley had combined nearly 30 years in the beer industry working for Miller Brewing before they opened their Loggerhead brewpub in 1990.

The brewpub is named after the loggerhead sea turtle which nests at some of North Carolina's remote beaches. Appropriate sea turtle artifacts decorate the brewpub.

Live music is featured on weekends.

Loggerhead sells draft kegs in the Greensboro, Winston-Salem, and High Point areas.

Brewpub menu: *pubfare*

Loggerhead Pilsner
Gate City Ale
General Greene Lager
Loggerhead Light

1991:   812 barrels
1992:   903 barrels
1993:   860 barrels

MILL BAKERY, BREWERY, AND EATERY
122 W. Woodlawn
Charlotte, NC 28217   704-525-5230

President: Jim Bostick
Brewer: Jason McKnight
Equipment:
Opened: April 16, 1993

The South has always prided itself on locally grown foods, southern recipes leaning heavily to fried foods, and plenty of barbecue. But the South is also becoming more health conscious. An example of this attention to heart-healthy foods is the Mill Bakery, Brewery, and Eatery, a chain of family restaurants throughout the Southeast. Almost a dozen brewpubs were planned for the Mill chain, but now the number is only three in Florida and one in North Carolina. Karl Strauss was the brewing consultant.

The trademark for the 125-seat restaurant is a paddle wheel at the front entrance. Fresh pastries and breads, many made with beer in the recipe, are a specialty of the bakery. Breakfasts are also served.

The Mill's four beers are available only on draft at the brewpub. Gallon "growlers" are in the plans for take-home trade. The Mill is one of two Charlotte brewpubs, the other being Dilworth Brewing. With a bustling economy, several colleges in the area, and the NBA Hornets franchise and a new NFL team coming, Charlotte is a likely to become a hub for craft brewing in North Carolina.

Brewpub menu: *complete lunches and dinners, with pizza and pasta specialties*

Harvest Gold Light
Red October
Hornet's Tail Ale
McKnight's Stout

1991:   **300 barrels**
1992:   **500 barrels**
1993:   **N/A**

≈ SPRING GARDEN BREWING
714 Francis King Street
Greensboro, NC 27410   910-219-3649

President: Bill Sherrill
Brewer: Christian Boos
Equipment: 10-barrel German brewhouse
Opened: March 12, 1991

The Spring Garden Brewpub is part of the Sherrill family chain of restaurants in central North Carolina. Owner Bill Sherrill, a graduate of Cornell's hotel management program, visited breweries all over the country in the 1980s before he felt he understood the industry well enough to try it back in North Carolina.

Sherrill opened Spring Garden Brewery at one of his restaurants in 1991 and hired Christian Boos, a Canadian brewer educated at the Weihenstephan Technical Brewing Institute. Sherrill instructed him to make lighter beers than Sherrill had found on his brewpub travels. Spring Garden's Hummin' Bird come in at less than 3% alcohol which Sherrill believes is what the younger beer drinkers prefer in North Carolina. Sherill's approach is to give the consumer what he or she wants and not try to make them like what the brewer wants to make.

Spring Garden brewpub has an interesting collection of antiques and collectibles Sherrill has picked up on his travels. Southwestern artwork, antique brewing equipment, and a 1940 New Delhi fire-engine red motorcycle are some of the prominent artifacts. Blues music is featured on Wednesday nights.

A $50,000 brewery expansion in 1993 increased capacity so that the five other Spring Garden Bar and Grills could serve the brewery's beers.

Brewpub menu: *ribs, seafood, pastas, and grilled specialties*

Hummin' Bird: *a light lager*
Red Oak Lager: *a Vienna-style lager*
Battlefield Black: *a dark lager*
Blackbeard Bock
Oktoberfest

1991: 1,500 barrels
1992: 1,000 barrels
1993: 1,500 barrels

~ TOISNOT BREWING/SPUR STEAKHOUSE
513 N. Ward Blvd.
Wilson, NC   919-237-0086

Co-owners: Andrew Etheridge, Scott & Sarah Bowers
Brewer: Scott Bowers
Equipment: 2-barrel system from Elliott Bay Metal
Opened: January 1, 1994

The Spur Steakhouse became North Carolina's eighth brewpub when the Toisnot Brewery sold its first beer on January 1, 1994. The Toisnot Brewery is named after the Toisnot Reservoir from which Wilson draws its water. Toisnot is the Indian word for the Great Dismal Swamp, a primordial wetlands on the North Carolina/Virginia border. The area is covered with scrub pines and wetland swamps leading to local legends about swamp creatures and giant snakes snatching farm animals and pets in the dark of the night.

Scott Bowers says he had been homebrewing with the "tea-stained" water from the Toisnot Reservoir for years. He says the soft Toisnot swamp water, with its high tannic acid and low pH factor, is almost perfect for making ales. It also makes for interesting public relations opportunities.

Scott and Sarah Bowers and Andrew Etheridge opened the Spur Steakhouse & Saloon in 1992, intending to add a brewery when permits and licenses were approved. The Spur prides itself on its large-screen TV for watching sporting events, a major pastime in North Carolina. Live entertainment and a monthly comedy club are featured on the second-floor dining area.

Brewpub menu: *mesquite grilled steaks, Tex-Mex specialties*

TBC Pale Ale
TBC India Pale Ale

TBC Porter
TBC Brown Ale
TBC Stout
TBC Black and Tan

 TUMBLEWEED GRILLE & BREWERY
122 Blowing Rock Road
Boone, NC 28607   704-264-7111

President: Bart Conway
Brewers: Cam Hedrick & Kinney Baughman
Equipment: 4-barrel homebrew designed system
Opened: May 1992

Bart Conway had a nice little southwestern restaurant in Boone, North Carolina when he decided to bring a little of the craft brewing world into this small, western Appalachian town. Conway had bought an old gas station/liquor store and converted it into a neo-adobe restaurant one might expect to find along a New Mexico highway.

When Conway came up with his idea to add a small brewery, he was fortunate to find a couple of seasoned home-brewers to help him. Brewer Cam Hedrick, a master woodworker, discovered fresh beers in Europe in the 1980s. He began homebrewing and became a professional when he was hired by Kinney Baughman in May 1992. Baughman was also a homebrewer who similarly discovered beer while traveling in Belgium in 1981. When he returned to North Carolina, he set up his own homebrewing company. In addition to brewery duties, Baughman works part-time as a philosophy instructor at Appalachian State University in Boone.

Brewing at Tumbleweed is carried out on used kitchen equipment put together in a rented house behind the restaurant. After fermentation and aging, the beer is carried down the hill in 5-gallon kegs to hook up to Tumbleweed's taps. Tumbleweed's brewing capacity has grown from a tiny 5-gallon homebrewing system in February 1992 to a 30-gallon system, to a

2-barrel, and finally a 4-barrel system. Four of their beers are on tap at one time. Tumbleweed also sells one-liter bottles for the take-home trade.

Brewpub menu: *grilled Mexican-southwestern specialties.*

Tumbleweed's Original Gold
Tumbleweed's Light Golden Ale
Tumbleweed's Amber Pale Ale
Tumbleweed's Wheat
Tumbleweed's Brewer's Reserve Stout
Tumbleweed's Steam Beer
Tumbleweed's Smoked Porter
Tumbleweed's Cherry Bock

1992:   N/A
1993:   120 barrels

 WEEPING RADISH BREWERY
Highway 64 on Roanoke Island
Manteo, NC 27954   919-473-1157

President: Uli Bennewitz
Brewer: Paul Hummer, Jay Fischer
Equipment: 15-barrel Bavarian brew house
Opened: July 4, 1986

Manteo is on North Carolina's Outer Banks, a popular resort famous for beautiful beaches, a sea bird sanctuary, and destructive hurricanes. The first colony in the New World was organized and settled by Sir Walter Raleigh on Roanoke Island in 1586. However, when ships from England arrived with supplies in 1588, no survivors were found. The settlers became known as the Lost Colony of Croatan from an inscription on a tree.

The Weeping Radish brewpub on Roanoke Island opened in 1986 as one of the first Big East brewpubs. Co-owners Eddie Greene and Richard

Lacerre owned the very successful Island Gallery and Christmas Shop in Manteo that sells Christmas goods to tourists year round. In 1984, they met Uli Bennewitz, a German businessman working in North Carolina, who wanted to start a craft brewery. They combined their resources and built a 5,000 sq. ft. Bavarian Gasthaus adjacent to the Island Gallery and Christmas Shop in 1986.

Weeping Radish's name refers to the German beer hall custom of peeling a white German radish in a spiral, sprinkling salt on it, and putting it back together. The salt draws moisture out of the radish making it appear as if it is weeping.

The food served in the 146-seat Weeping Radish is imported from Germany, and recipes are prepared by German chefs. Kartoffelsuppe, Wiener schnitzel, jagerschnitzel, sauerbraten, and wursts are offered along with American standard steaks, chicken, and seafood prepared from German recipes. The waitresses wear bright-colored German dresses, white aprons, and bows in their hair. All of Weeping Radish's beers are, of course, brewed according to the Bavarian Reinheitsbegot which permits only barley, hops, yeast, and water in brewing.

Weeping Radish has all the features one might expect of a Bavarian beer hall – a ginger bread-style house, beer garden, playground for children, outdoor patio, clock tower, and courtyard with shops and an art gallery. In 1993, the Weeping Radish went through an expansion to 1,500 barrels/year to allow for off-premise sale of mini-kegs, returnable liter "growlers," and 22-oz bottles. Distribution will include southern Virginia and the cities of Norfolk, Richmond, and Charlottesville.

Weeping Radish has the advantages of brewing at a separate facility in Durham that was the Weeping Radish #2. The brewpub went through ownership changes and became the Old Heidelberg brewery and later a restaurant. The restaurant closed in 1993 but brewing operation continued to supply beer for the Manteo Weeping Radish. The arrangement is allowed under an ATF regulation on controlled brewing for a brewery to ship beer in bond under one license. This makes two 15-barrel breweries working at near capacity to meet the demand for Weeping Radish's beers.

Brewpub menu: *a combination of authentic German food and American dishes*

Weeping Radish Helles: *a light lager*
Weeping Radish Fest Bier: *amber lager*
The Black Radish: *a dark, creamy lager*

1991:   700 barrels
1992:   884 barrels
1993:   1,335 barrels

PALMETTO BREWING
289 Huger Street
Charleston, SC 29403   803-884-0699

Owners: Louis Bruce & Ed Falkenstein
Brewer: Louis Bruce
Equipment: 10-barrel Newlands system
Opened: May 1994

Louis Bruce and Ed Falkenstein met in the early 1990s while wind surfing in the Columbia Gorge between Oregon and Washington. After sampling the local Oregon beers, the two South Carolinians came up with a plan to bring craft beers back home.

Falkenstein is a chemical engineer working in Spartanburg. Bruce had worked for a wine distributor and paving company. They pooled their talents, researched the brewing industry, found a distributor in South Carolina, and came up with a business plan. They quit their respective jobs, got a bank loan, and found a site in Huger Street. The Palmetto Brewery is in an abandoned warehouse once used by the Navy in the old part of Charleston.

Charleston has a bustling tourism business for those seeking the Old South experience of plantations, mint juleps, grits, and country ham. Bruce and Falkenstein hope that tourists and residents alike will find a local craft beer part of the authentic southern experience. They will begin with a single beer, Palmetto Amber, that will be sold principally in bottles.

Palmetto Amber

⇒ BIBLIOGRAPHY ⇐

Anderson, Will. *Beer, USA.* Morgan & Morgan, Dobbs Ferry, New York, 1986.

–––. *Beer, New England.* Will Anderson, Portland, Maine, 1988.

Asbury, Herbert. *The Great Illusion: An Informal History of Prohibition.* Doubleday & Company, Garden City, N.Y., 1950.

Baron, Stanley. *Brewed in America: A History of Beer and Ale in the United States.* Little Brown & Company, Boston, 1962.

Earle, Alice Morse. *Customs and Fashions in Old New England.* Charles E. Tuttle Company, Rutland, Vermont, 1973.

Ehret, George. *Twenty-Five Years of Brewing.* New York, 1891.

Lender, Mark Edward & Martin, James Kirby. *Drinking in America: A History.* The Free Press, New York, 1982.

One Hundred Years of Brewing. Chicago & New York, 1903.

Rorabaugh, W. J. *The Alcoholic Republic.* Oxford University Press, New York & Oxford, 1979.

≈ INDEX ≈

A

Acadia/Lompoc   57
Adams, John   17
Adams, Samuel   15
Ale Street News   iv, 44, 47
All About Beer   iv, 49
Allegheny/Pennsylvania
   139-40
Anchor   i, 79
Andrews   58
Anheuser-Busch   iv, 28, 32-33,
   39, 110, 186
Atlantic Coast   67-68
Arrowhead   140-141

B

Baltimore   107-108, 113
Bardo Rodeo   157-159, 163
Bar Harbor   58-59
BarleyCorn   iv, 44, 47
Beach   171, 177
Beer Institute   iii
Bergner & Engel   30, 35
Blue Ridge   159-160

Boston Beer Company   iii, 2,
   68-72, 147-148
Boston Beer Works   72-74
Brooklyn   118-119
Brown & Moran   119-120
Buffalo   122-123
Buffalo/Abbot Square
   121-122
Buffalo Bill's   i

C

California, University of-Davis
   55, 109, 160, 182
Cambridge   74
Cape Cod   75
Capitol City   111, 167-168
Casco Bay   59
Catamount
   53, 85, 91, 93, 95-96, 99,
   117, 183
Commonwealth   2, 76-77, 95
   179

W

Y

Z

Yes, I would like to order books from RedBrick Press.

Brewery Adventures in the Big East	0-941397-06-8	$14.95	_____
California Brewin'	0-941397-05-X	$11.95	_____
Brewery Adventures in the Wild West	0-941397-04-1	$14.95	_____
Star Spangled Beer: A Guide to America's New Microbreweries and Brewpubs	0-941397-00-9	$13.95	_____
Great Cooking with Beer	0-941397-01-7	$10.95	_____

California Residents Add Sales Tax (7.5%) _____

(International orders add $5.00 U.S.)   Shipping ($1.50/book) _____

TOTAL _____

☐ Please send information on RedBrick's books on specialty beers.

Name _____

Address _____

City _____ State _____ Zip _____

RedBrick Press
P.O. Box 1895 • Sonoma, California 95476

- -

Yes, I would like to order books from RedBrick Press.

Brewery Adventures in the Big East	0-941397-06-8	$14.95	_____
California Brewin'	0-941397-05-X	$11.95	_____
Brewery Adventures in the Wild West	0-941397-04-1	$14.95	_____
Star Spangled Beer: A Guide to America's New Microbreweries and Brewpubs	0-941397-00-9	$13.95	_____
Great Cooking with Beer	0-941397-01-7	$10.95	_____

California Residents Add Sales Tax (7.5%) _____

(International orders add $5.00 U.S.)   Shipping ($1.50/book) _____

TOTAL _____

☐ Please send information on RedBrick's books on specialty beers.

Name _____

Address _____

City _____ State _____ Zip _____

RedBrick Press
P.O. Box 1895 • Sonoma, California 95476